Milady's Standard Esthetics: Advanced Student Workbook

Milady

CENGAGE
Learning™

Australia • Brazil • Japan • Korea • Mexico • Singapore • Spain • United Kingdom • United States

Milady's Standard Esthetics: Advanced Student Workbook, First Edition

Jean Harrity

President, Milady: Dawn Gerrain

Publisher: Erin O'Connor

Acquisitions Editor: Martine Edwards

Product Manager: Jessica Burns

Editorial Assistant: Elizabeth Edwards

Director of Beauty Industry Relations: Sandra Bruce

Senior Marketing Manager: Gerard McAvey

Marketing Specialist: Erica Conley

Production Director: Wendy Troeger

Content Project Manager: Angela Iula

Senior Art Director: Joy Kocsis

For product information and technology assistance, contact us at **Professional & Career Group Customer Support, 1-800-648-7450**

For permission to use material from this text or product, submit all requests online at **www.cengage.com/permissions.** Further permissions questions can be e-mailed to **permissionrequest@cengage.com.**

Library of Congress Control Number: 2009900257

ISBN-13: 978-1-4283-1977-6

ISBN-10: 1-4283-1977-8

Milady
5 Maxwell Drive
Clifton Park, NY 12065-2919
USA

Cengage Learning products are represented in Canada by Nelson Education, Ltd.

For your lifelong learning solutions, visit **milady.cengage.com**

Visit our corporate website at **www.cengage.com**

Notice to the Reader

Publisher does not warrant or guarantee any of the products described herein or perform any independent analysis in connection with any of the product information contained herein. Publisher does not assume, and expressly disclaims, any obligation to obtain and include information other than that provided to it by the manufacturer. The reader is expressly warned to consider and adopt all safety precautions that might be indicated by the activities described herein and to avoid all potential hazards. By following the instructions contained herein, the reader willingly assumes all risks in connection with such instructions. The publisher makes no representations or warranties of any kind, including but not limited to, the warranties of fitness for particular purpose or merchantability, nor are any such representations implied with respect to the material set forth herein, and the publisher takes no responsibility with respect to such material. The publisher shall not be liable for any special, consequential, or exemplary damages resulting, in whole or part, from the readers' use of, or reliance upon, this material.

Printed in the United States of America
3 4 5 12 11 10

Milady's Standard Esthetics: Advanced Student Workbook

How to use this Workbook

This Workbook is designed to accompany Milady's Standard Esthetics: Advanced. The exercise in each chapter, which follow the content in the textbook, are meant to test simple recall and reasoning and to reinforce your understanding of the information.

Exercise range from fill-in-the-blank questions, true/false, matching, to more challenging word puzzles, as well as discussion questions that encourage you to apply theoretial knowledge to real-life situations. You may wish to write your answers in pencil, either relying on memory or consulting the textbook. Items may be corrected and rated during class or in discussion sessions with other students, or you may decide to use this workbook for independent study.

We hope that you enjoy using this workbook and that it gives you a comprehensive, study tool for learning about the world of professional skin care.

CHANGES IN ESTHETICS

Date: _____

Rating: _____

Text Pages: 3–17

INTRODUCTION

Answer the following questions.

1. Why are estheticians in great demand? _____
    _____

2. A demand for well educated estheticians has grown and expanded into the _____
    _____

3. What generation has had a huge effect on the skin care industry? _____
    _____ Why? _____
    _____

THE GLOBAL EVOLUTION OF SPAS AND SPA TREATMENTS

Answer the following questions.

1. How does understanding the history of the spa and spa treatments help the esthetician?
    _____

2. Explain two possible origins of the word *spa*.

    a) _____
        _____
    b) _____
        _____

3. Match each of the following words or phrases to its meaning:

    a. _____ *"sanitas per aquas"*   1. Fountain

    b. _____ *spagere*   2. Health through water

    c. _____ *espa*   3. To scatter, sprinkle, moisten

4. Name the three water treatments provided in the spa.

a) _____

b) _____

c) _____

5. Before evolving toward the use of baths for relaxation, what was the focus of the Roman bathing culture? _____

6. Name the three types of Roman bath houses: _____

7. What was the purpose of bloodletting? _____

8. During the seventeenth century, the French used _____ springs for drinking cures as well as for _____ and they used _____ springs only for _____.

9. What did the Bavarian monk, Father Sebastian Kneipp, believe water could be use for? _____

10. Why did the popularity of spa treatments, such as health and exercise regiments, mud therapy, and balneology, lose ground in the 1900s? _____

11. Today Americans are flocking to spas for _____ and much more.

ADVANCED EDUCATION AND EMPLOYMENT OPPORTUNITIES

Answer the following questions.

1. Match the following job type with its definition.

_____ esthetician

1. duties might include keeping records of sales and inventory on hand, demonstrating products, selling to clients, and running the cash register

_____ makeup artist

2. educates clients in the benefits of various cosmetic lines

_____ permanent makeup artist

3. a buyer of cosmetics in a department store, specialty store, or salon

_____ medical esthetician

_____ manufacturer/sales representative

_____ department store cosmetics representative

_____ cosmetic buyer or assistant buyer

_____ manager or salesperson

_____ state licensing inspector or examiner

4. specializes in the care of the skin

5. artfully applies cosmetics

6. trained in cosmetic tattooing

7. esthetician partnered with a dermatologist or plastic surgeon

8. prepares and conducts examinations, announces and enforces rules and regulations, investigates complaints, and conducts hearings

9. explains, demonstrates, and sells products

2. What are the most common services offered in permanent cosmetics? _____

_____

3. What can esthetics instructors do to keep up to date on their knowledge? _____

_____

4. A _____ has the same qualities as a salesperson but assumes more responsibility.

5. If you have talent in writing or journalism, what type of career may you wish to pursue?

_____

DEVELOPING CRITICAL-THINKING SKILLS

Answer the following questions.

1. List the steps for developing critical-thinking, problem-solving, and decision-making skills:

a. _____

b. _____

c. _____

d. _____

e. _____

2. What is a popular method of documenting the critical-thinking process? _____
List and explain the acronym.

a. _____

b. _____

c. _____

d. _____

ENHANCING SOFT SKILLS

Answer the following questions.

1. _____ thought revolves around the idea of treating the person as a whole rather than focusing solely on a disease or disorder.

2. List some of the ways you can release yourself from negativity and distractedness.

a. _____

b. _____

c. _____

d. _____

e. _____

f. _____

3. List the eight steps to manage negative emotions:

a. _____

b. _____

c. _____

d. _____

e. _____

f. _____

g. _____

h. _____

PRIVACY LAWS

List the key standards of patient protection.

1. _____

2. _____

3. _____

4. _____

5. _____

6. _____

7. _____

8. _____

2 INFECTION CONTROL

Date: _____

Rating: _____

Text Pages: 19–52

RULES AND REGULATIONS GOVERNING WORKPLACE SAFETY

Answer the following questions.

1. Write out what each acronym stands for:

   AIDS _____

   CDC _____

   EPA _____

   FDA _____

   HIV _____

   HBV _____

   OSHA _____

   PPE _____

2. What is the Bloodborne Pathogens Standard?

   _____

   _____

   _____

   _____

3. Give a brief description of each item.

   a. Universal and Standard Precautions:

   _____

   _____

   _____

b. Engineering controls and work practice controls:

_____

_____

_____

c. Personal protective equipment:

_____

_____

_____

d. Cleanliness of work areas:

_____

_____

_____

_____

e. Hepatitis B vaccine:

_____

_____

_____

_____

_____

_____

f. Follow-up after exposure:

_____

_____

_____

_____

HEPATITIS

Answer the following questions.

1. What does *hepatitis* mean? _____

    Match the various types of hepatitis with the descriptions by putting the number of the description next to the type of hepatitis. There may be more then one response.

    _____ Hepatitis A

    _____ Hepatitis B

    _____ Hepatitis C

_____ Hepatitis E

_____ Hepatitis G

_____ Hepatitis I

1. HIV

2. Transmitted via contact with contaminated food

3. A vaccine is available

4. Can be contracted by kissing

5. Caused by poor sanitation

6. Occurs in 25% of patients with Hepatitis A

7. Occurs in 20% of patients with Hepatitis C

8. Kills or impairs the immune cells

9. Was identified only a few years ago

MICROBIOLOGY

Unscramble each word using the clues.

1. blmcigooyiro   _____   The science that studies microscopic organisms

2. ornmla frloa   _____   Resident microorganism

3. sdpoamnsueo   _____   A type of resident microorganism

4. trsenntai crmogsminorais   _____   They are easily picked up on hands, clothing, and other inanimate objects.

5. negathpos   _____   Organisms that cause disease

6. yphcclistaooc   _____   A type of resident microorganism

BACTERIA, VIRUSES, FUNGI, AND PARASITES

Label each bacteria and then answer the questions below.

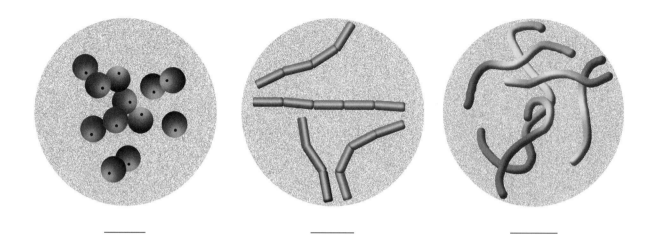

_____   _____   _____

1. Which bacteria do not cause harm to humans? _____
_____

2. Is a virus bigger or smaller then bacteria? _____
_____

3. List a few viruses. _____
_____

4. What are molds and yeasts a form of? _____
_____

5. How do parasites function? _____
_____
_____

6. List three types of parasites. _____
_____

7. When can nosocomial infections appear? _____
_____
_____

8. Give an example of a nosocomial infection. _____
_____
_____

Solve the puzzle with terms from the chapter.

Across
6. A portal of exit.
7. It occurs when the residue of evaporated droplets from an infected person remains in the air long enough to be transmitted.

Down
1. A microorganism with the ability to spread infection. (2 words)
2. Contact with animal, insect or parasite.
3. Person to person contact.
4. Is another portal of exit.
5. Is a main route for a disease to be transmitted.

ASEPTIC TECHNIQUE AS APPLIED TO ESTHETICS
_____

Answer the following questions.

1. What are the two techniques that are used for aseptic control? _____

_____

2. What are the five keys of asepsis?

a. _____

b. _____

c. _____

d. _____

e. _____

3. What is the definition of *sterile*?

   _____

4. Sterilized items can include:

   _____

   _____

5. What are two benefits of hand washing?

   a. _____

   b. _____

6. List 11 times when someone should wash their hands.

   a. _____

   b. _____

   c. _____

   d. _____

   e. _____

   f. _____

   g. _____

   h. _____

   i. _____

   j. _____

   k. _____

7. List two ingredients an antiseptic agent should contain:

   a. _____

   b. _____

8. Put the following list in the proper order:

_____ Use a clean paper towel to turn off the faucet.

_____ Vigorously rub together all surfaces of lathered hands.

_____ Blot hands dry with a disposable paper towel.

_____ Wet your hands with warm running water.

_____ Apply soap.

_____ Thoroughly rinse your hands.

_____ Optional: Apply hand lotion.

GLOVES

Answer the following questions.

1. List the types of gloves that are on the market.

   a. _____

   b. _____

   c. _____

   d. _____

   e. _____

2. What are some good points for natural rubber latex (NRL)?

   a. _____

   b. _____

   c. _____

   d. _____

3. What is a drawback for natural rubber latex? _____

4. What are the benefits of nitrile gloves?

   a. _____

   b. _____

   c. _____

5. How can you tell if the material that your gloves are made of is breaking down?

a. _____

b. _____

c. _____

d. _____

e. _____

f. _____

g. _____

EQUIPMENT

Put the following list in the proper order:

_____ Inspect equipment for any residual debris.

_____ Place equipment in a disinfecting tub filled with an EPA-registered disinfectant.

_____ Rinse equipment.

_____ Package equipment with indicators dated for the day of autoclaving.

_____ Place packets ready for sterilization where they will be readily accessible for sterilization process but not where they will become wet.

_____ Thoroughly scrub equipment under water to remove any visible gross debris.

_____ Clean work area

_____ Rinse equipment and pat dry.

_____ Ensure that all equipment packages and indicators are properly marked.

_____ Rinse equipment and pat dry.

DECONTAMINATION

Answer the following questions.

1. What is the definition of *decontamination*? _____
   _____

2. What are detergents? _____
   _____

3. The effectiveness of a disinfectant also depends on other factors, including:

   a. _____

   b. _____

   c. _____

   d. _____

   e. _____

   f. _____

   g. _____

   h. _____

4. Instruments used on clients in a body modification procedure are divided into three
   categories based on the degree of infection risk when the items were used on clients.
   Describe each category.

   a. Critical items: _____
   _____
   _____

   b. Semi-critical items: _____
   _____
   _____

   c. Non-critical items: _____
   _____

5. Describe the levels of disinfection:

   a. High-level disinfection: _____
   _____
   _____

b. Intermediate-level disinfection: _____

_____

c. Low-level disinfection: _____

_____

STEAM STERILIZATION

Answer the following questions.

1. What are the four key things to watch when using an autoclave? _____

_____

2. What do indicators respond to? _____

3. What do integrators respond to? _____

4. What should you refer to when using an autoclave? _____

POTENTIAL HAZARDS FOR AN ESTHETICIAN

Answer the following questions.

1. What is an example of a sharp implement that can cause a needlestick? _____

2. What should immediately happen after a needlestick occurs? _____

3. What are the three steps in a screen exposure?

_____

_____

_____

4. What should you look for when inspecting your hands?

_____

5. The training received at a medical facility may include the following:

_____

_____

6. List the basic safety guidelines:

a. _____

b. _____

c. _____

3 ADVANCED HISTOLOGY OF THE CELL AND THE SKIN

Date: _____

Rating: _____

Text Pages: 53–86

CELLULAR STRUCTURE AND FUNCTION

Answer the following questions.

1. What does an understanding of the histology and the physiology of the skin provide?

    _____

    _____

2. All cells have the same components, but they differentiate themselves to fulfill different

    _____ .

3. Describe selective permeability. _____

    _____

4. A cellular membrane is not a single thickness but rather a _____ which is two layers of lipid with water sandwiched in between.

5. _____ make up the lipid bilayer and give the cell its globe-like three-dimensional form.

6. _____ are the communication system between different cells, tissues, and organs and all parts of the body.

7. Where do receptors receive messages from? _____

8. Production of sebum in the sebaceous gland is stimulated by _____ that are received by the receptor sites in the cells of the sebaceous gland.

9. Small structures within the cell that each have their own function are known as

    _____ .

10. The structure located inside the cell cytoplasm is called the _____ .

11. Small organelles that help build protein structures from a set of genetic instructions are known as _____ and are the protein "construction division" of the _____ .

12. The "lungs" and "digestive system" of the cell are known as _____ and are the energy producers.

13. The _____ apparatus is a storage mechanism that helps store proteins for later conversion.

14. The "demolition crew" of the cell, the _____, manufacture enzymes. Describe what these enzymes do. _____

_____

15. Describe the purpose of the vacuoles: _____

_____

16. Identify each section of the picture below.

17. The brain of the cell, similar to the central processing unit on your computer, is the

_____.

18. _____ within the nucleus are responsible for cellular division.

A BRIEF REVIEW OF SKIN STRUCTURE

Answer the following questions.

1. What is the largest organ of the body? _____

2. The two major layers of the skin are the _____.

3. Describe the epidermis:

a. _____

b. _____

4. How does the dermis differ from the epidermis? _____

5. List the functions of the skin:

a. _____

_____

b. _____

c. _____

d. _____

e. _____

f. _____

g. _____

MAJOR CELLS IN THE DERMIS

Answer the following questions.

1. What is the major cell in the skin? _____

2. The keratinocyte begins as a _____ , also known as a mother cell. It is capable of dividing many times and forming new cells called _____.

3. Keratin proteins make up part of the _____ , which is the support structure in the cell.

4. What are the three main fibers that make up the cytoskeleton:

a. _____

b. _____

c. _____

5. The melanocyte is a cell in the _____ of the epidermis. What does it produce?

_____

6. What is the name of the process that produces melanin? _____

7. Damaged DNA produces _____ fragments, which triggers release of the MSH.

8. What provides the skin's color? _____

9.   What are most skin-lightening agents designed to block and prevent? _____

_____

10. List the safe agents used for skin lightening:

a.   _____

b.   _____

c.   _____

d.   _____

e.   _____

f.   _____

MAJOR CELLS IN THE DERMIS

Answer the following questions.

1.   What is the most abundant protein in the body called? _____ *What makes this protein?* _____

2.   Describe the origin of the fibroblast. _____

_____

3.   What are fibroblasts? _____

4.   What do mast cells appear to be involved in? _____ *Explains what occurs:*

_____

_____

5.   *Leukocyte* means _____ .

6.   Name the two major types of white cells:

a.   _____

b.   _____

7.   How do granulocytes get their name? _____

_____

8.   Identify the stain color for each of the following blood cells:

a.   Neutrophils _____

   b. Eosinophils _____

   c. Basophils _____

9. Which type of blood cell is the most abundant type of white blood cell and the most important part of the immune system?_____

10. What is another name for granulocytes? _____

11. The life span of a neutrophil blood cell is _____

_____

12. Which white blood cells are specific for parasitic infections in the body? _____

_____

13. Eosinophils stay in circulation for _____ *hours but can survive for* _____

days.

14. What do basophils do? _____

_____.

15. List the secretions of basophils:

   a. _____

   b. _____

   c. _____

16. The main factor that triggers repair of the stratum corneum is _____

17. _____ *provide a barrier between the individual and the environment.*

18. Where are keratinocyte stem cells located? _____

19. Describe the spinous layer. _____

_____

20. What is the major protein formed within keratinocytes? _____

21. The congenital disease known as _____ *develops because of defects in*

keratins 5 and 14 in the _____

PROTEINS OF THE DERMIS—THE EXTRACELLULAR MATRIX (ECM)

Answer the following questions.

1. The most abundant protein in the body is _____ . *What is it made by?*

   _____

2. Elastin is an important protein for:

   a. _____

   b. _____

   c. _____

   d. _____

   e. _____

   f. _____

3. _____ consist of a protein and a complex sugar called a polysaccharide.

4. What is the major function of versican? _____

   _____

5. The proteoglycans maintain _____ in the dermas, provide support for other dermal components, and all function as a matrix for _____ .

THE CELL CYCLE

Answer the following questions.

1. The final state of growth in cell division is called _____ .

2. Identify each of the following bases with its correct abbreviation.

   a. adenine _____

   b. thymine _____

   c. guanine _____

   d. cytosine _____

3. A series of enzymes called _____ control much of the process of cell division.

4. How are the epidermis and the dermis regulated? _____

_____

AN INTRODUCTION TO EMBRYOLOGY—THE STEM CELL

Answer the following questions.

1. The study of the very early stages of development after fertilization of any living organism is known as _____.

2. The fertilized egg is called a _____ and it goes through a series of rapid cell divisions at what is called the _____ stage.

3. The three germ layers in the gastrula process are referred to as:

   a. _____

   b. _____

   c. _____

4. The ectoderm germ layer has _____ and produces many tissues and cells.

5. What does the external ectoderm supply? _____

_____

6. What is the neural crest often called? _____

7. The neural tube provides most of the _____.

8. What comes from the mesoderm stem cell?

   a. _____

   b. _____

   c. _____

   d. _____

   e. _____

   f. _____

   g. _____

9. _____ forms the epithelial lining of the digestive tube.

10. The cells of the ectoderm, mesoderm, and endoderm make up the true _____.

THE MAJOR TISSUES IN THE BODY

1. The body organs are built of _____ *basic tissues. Name them:*

   a. _____

   b. _____

   c. _____

   d. _____

2. Match each of the following tissues with its correct description.

   a. _____ muscle tissue

   b. _____ epithelial tissue

   c. _____ muscle tissue

   d. _____ connective tissue

   1. Separates the underlying organs or tissues from the external environment

   2. Provides functions of mechanical reinforcement, transport, and diffusion of nutrients and wastes

   3. A highly specialized tissue that is used to transport signals to other organs

   4. Provides movement for the body and derives from mesoderm

THE BASIC IMMUNE SYSTEM

Answer the following questions.

1. An elaborate defense mechanism that the body uses to determine self from non-self is the _____ *system.*

2. Any material that elicits an immune response is called an _____.

3. The body's defense against antigens is _____.

4. What are the two major parts of the immune system?

   a. _____

   b. _____

5. The active cell in the cell-mediated immunity is the _____. What does the T stand for? _____

6. Cytotoxic or killer T cells do their work by releasing _____, *which cause* _____.

7. _____ T cells serve as managers, directing the immune response.

8. Suppressor T cells inhibit the production of _____ T cells.

9. What are memory T cells programmed to do? _____

    _____

10. Skin cells contain _____, which are enzymes that destroy bacteria by rupturing their cell walls.

MECHANISM OF EXFOLIATION—THE DESMOSOMES

Answer the following questions.

1. There are at least four types of cellular bonds within the _____.

2. What do tight junctions possibly serve as? _____

3. Tight junctions prevent _____ from entering a cell unless there is _____ for a particular kind of protein.

4. What do adherens junctions provide? _____

    _____

5. What do Gap junctions provide? _____

    _____

6. The _____ is the major structure that holds the epidermal cells together and in particular the cells of the _____.

7. What are the two plates or plaques located in the cell membrane?

    a. _____

    b. _____

8. The _____ bind the basal layer to the basement membrane through different types of proteins.

9. How much of the stratum corneum is lost each day? _____

10. Enzymes are packaged in the lamellar bodies of the stratum granulosum in an inactive form called _____ .

11. When you wish to exfoliate the stratum corneum, what kind of agent must be used?

_____

12. A superficial peel that is about 10 cell layers deep in the stratum corneum will take less than _____ to heal.

SKIN PENETRATION AND PERMEATION

Answer the following questions.

1. Explain what the barrier of the skin controls. _____

_____

2. The pH of the skin is important for barrier _____ .

3. Scientists believe that the pH functions to keep the enzymes functioning at the proper level of _____ .

4. Proper acid pH is about 5.5, which is the level needed to maintain _____ on the skin.

5. What is a good way to remove skin lipids? _____

SENSORY NERVES AND PERCEPTION IN THE SKIN

Answer the following questions.

1. What is the facial nerve? _____

2. The main sensory nerve in the face is the _____ , also known as the

_____ .

3. Name the three main divisions of the trigeminal nerve:

a. _____

b. _____

c. _____

4. The _____ is the part of the nervous system that is known as the peripheral nervous system.

5. Name the two parts to the reflex arcs:

   a. _____

   b. _____

6. What are the two major functional divisions of the ANS? _____

7. The sympathetic division may be considered the _____ part and the parasympathetic division is the _____ .

8. _____ are single fibers that join at the hair bulb and wrap around the end of the hair in fine body hair.

9. _____ refer to a nerve that occurs in glabrous or hairless skin.

10. The _____ is found in frictional areas of the skin, such as the hands, fingers, and soles of the foot.

11. The _____ occur in the deep part of the dermis of the palms and fingers near the bones.

12. _____ detect both heat and cold.

13. Where are the end-bulbs of Krause found? _____

    _____

14. Nerve endings in the subcutaneous tissue of the human finger are _____ .

4 HORMONES

Date: _____

Rating: _____

Text Pages: 87–102

WHAT ARE HORMONES?

Answer the following questions

1   _____ have very definite effects on the skin, and their function is directly related to many skin problems.

2.   The body undergoes hormonal changes due to _____.

3.   Hormones are _____ that are manufactured or secreted by glands within the body.

4.   Which types of glands secrete hormones? _____

THE ENDOCRINE GLANDS

Answer the following questions.

1.   How many major endocrine glands are there in the human body? _____

2.   Match the following gland with its description.

_____ pituitary gland   a. part of the immune system

_____ hypothalamus gland   b. located just above the kidneys

_____ thyroid gland   c. the ovaries in females and the testes in males

_____ parathyroid glands   d. connects the pituitary gland to the brain

_____ adrenal glands   e. Its function is not well understood, but it is
                                    thought to be related to the sex hormones.

_____ pineal gland   f. secretes trophic hormones

_____ thymus gland

_____ sex glands

g. regulates both cellular and body metabolism

h. are responsible for regulating calcium and phosphates in the bloodstream

3. Trophic hormones or _____ are chemicals that cause other glands to make other hormones.

4. The pituitary gland produces special hormones that cause:

a. _____

b. _____

c. _____

d. _____

5. The hypothalamus gland controls some involuntary muscles such as the _____

6. Where is the thyroid gland located? _____

7. _____ is one of the hormones secreted by the thyroid gland. Without it, _____ occurs in children.

8. Two hormones needed by the nervous system are _____ and _____

9. Which gland has a medulla and a cortex? _____

10. _____ could be called the emergency hormone and is secreted when the body is under stress.

11. Where is the pancreas located? _____

12. The specialized cells in the pancreas that produce insulin are called the _____

13. _____ is a disease that results from the pancreas not secreting enough insulin.

14. Which gland produces specialized lymphocytes to help the body fight disease?

_____

15. The male hormone responsible for development of typical male characteristics, such as a deep voice, broad shoulders, body hair, and other male characteristics, is _____ The female hormone that gives a woman female characteristics such as breasts and helps with the development of the menstrual cycle is _____

16. The _____ from the pituitary glands causes the testes to produce sperm, while the _____ causes the testes to manufacture testosterone.

17. Follice-stimulating hormones cause development of the _____ , while luteinizing hormones cause the actual process of _____

THE HORMONAL PHASES OF LIFE

Answer the following questions.

1. During puberty, the production of androgen begins and the _____ produce more sebum.

2. _____ is a sebaceous gland stimulant and its activity and production causes _____ of the follicles. Describe this dilation. _____

   _____

   _____

3. In addition, the _____ becomes oilier due to androgen production.

4. What instructions should be given to a young client for proper home care? _____

   _____

   _____

5. List the steps for in-salon treatments for young clients:

   a. _____

   b. _____

   _____

   c. _____

   d. _____

   e. _____

   f. _____

   g. _____

6. Keratosis pilaris is a problem often associated with _____ Describe how it appears _____ Describe how to treat it. _____

7. Describe a pregnancy mask. _____

   _____

8. What is the cause of a pregnancy mask? _____

   _____

9. Should hyperpigmentation be treated during pregnancy? _____

10. Stretch marks or _____ are marks that occur in pregnant women.

11. What can be used during pregnancy to help reduce the severity of stretch marks during pregnancy? _____

12. An increase in blood flow and blood pressure during pregnancy may lead to the development of _____. Describe this condition. _____
_____

13. Why do varicose veins develop during pregnancy? _____
_____

14. Explain why acne will often flare up after a woman gives birth or while nursing. _____
_____

15. What normal treatment should not be used to treat acne in pregnant women? _____
_____

16. Can most routine procedures be performed on pregnant women? _____

PREMENSTRUAL SYNDROME

Answer the following questions.

1. A condition in which some women experience uncomfortable physical changes before menstruation is known as _____

2. What is the best way to deal with PMS? _____

3. Seven to ten days before menstruation, women frequently experience _____

4. How should premenstrual acne be treated? _____
_____
_____

BIRTH CONTROL PILLS

Answer the following questions.

1. Birth control pills work by regulating _____ normally associated with the menstrual cycle.

2. Describe the two basic types of birth control pills.

   a. _____

   _____

   b. _____

   _____

3. A skin problem often associated with the use of birth control pills is the tendency to have

   _____

4. What type of birth control pills tend to be more aggravating to acne conditions? _____

   _____

5. Another appearance problem related to birth control pills is that of _____
   or melasma.

MENOPAUSE

Answer the following questions.

1. The time in a woman's life when the ovaries stop releasing ova is called _____
   Describe what happens. _____

2. As menopause occurs, _____ has a strong influence on collagen formation.

3. List what a lack of estrogen may affect:

   a. _____

   b. _____

   c. _____

   d. _____

   e. _____

4. Explain what causes hot flashes. _____

HIRSUTISM

Answer the following questions.

1. Hirsutism refers to _____. Who may experience this? _____

   _____

2. How is hirsutism treated?

a. _____

b. _____

c. _____

d. _____

OTHER HORMONAL DISORDERS THAT AFFECT THE SKIN

Answer the following questions.

1. A condition in which the thyroid gland secretes too much thyroid hormone is called

_____

2. Adrenal gland disorders can result in _____

3. A person with Cushing's syndrome secretes too much _____

5 **ANATOMY AND PHYSIOLOGY: MUSCLES AND NERVES**

Date: _____

Rating: _____

Text Pages: 103–120

MUSCLE TYPES FILL IN THE MISSING WORDS.

1. Muscle cells are referred to as _____.

2. _____ assists in the muscle's ability to contract and shorten.

3. The three different of muscle tissue are _____
   _____.

4. Cardiac muscles are a type of striated muscle and the contract _____.

5. Smooth also called striated and they contract _____.

6. Smooth muscles are found in hollow internal _____.

7. Smooth muscles can be found in the _____ and the _____.

8. Skeletal muscles are so called because they are attached to the _____.

9. Skeletal muscles operate _____.

10. The beginning point to a muscle is called the _____.

11. Several muscle fibers are bunched together and wrapped in a fibrous sheathing called a
    _____.

12. _____ is a type of neurotransmitter that crosses the synapse and is received on the other end.

13. The beginning point to a muscle is called the _____.

14. The more movable attachment of the muscle is called the _____.

15. The muscle that goes across the forehead is called the _____.

16. At the hairline, the Frontalis shades off into an _____.

17. The muscle that draws the eyebrows down and in is called the _____.

18. The largest muscles in the body are called the _____ muscles.

19. Individual muscle fibers are protected by connective tissue known as an _____.

20. The neurons branch out and meet muscle cells at a point called the _____

    _____.

SKELETAL MUSCLES

1. Matching

   A. Frontalis

   B. Aponeurosis

   C. Orbicularis Oculi

   D. Corrugator

   E. Quadratus Labii Superioris

   F. Orbicularis Oris

   G. Nasolabial Folds

   H. Procerus

   I. Sternocleidomastoid

   J. Platysma

   K. Pectoralis Major

   L. Intercostal Muscles

   M. Internal Obliques

   N. Trapezius

   O. Soleus

   P. Palpebra

   Q. Quadriceps

   1. _____ In the vertex of the skull

   2. _____ Located on the anterior of the thigh

   3. _____ Muscle in the upper lip

   4. _____ Muscle in the chest

   5. _____ Forehead muscle

   6. _____ Located at the back of leg

   7. _____ Around the mouth

   8. _____ Muscle of the nose

   9. _____ Muscle that rotates the head

   10. _____ Muscle originates in the chest

   11. _____ Eyelid, upper and lower

   12. _____ Makes up the majority of the upper back

   13. _____ They run angled to the traverse abdominal muscles

   14. _____ Draws eyebrows down and in

   15. _____ Around the eye

   16. _____ Muscles found in between the Ribs

   17. _____ Marionette lines

Name the function of the following terms.

2. Cardiac Muscle: _____

3. Neuron: _____

4. Insertion: _____

5. Frontalis: _____

6. Frowning Muscle: _____

7. Zygomaticus: _____

8. Deltoid: _____

9. Hamstrings: _____

10. Quadriceps: _____

MUSCLES OF THE FACE

1. Label the correct areas with the following muscles: corrugator, procerus, and pyramidalis nasi.

2. Name the 2 muscles of the neck: _____

3. Name 4 muscles of the abdomen: _____
_____

4. Name 2 muscles on the back: _____

5. Name 4 muscles of the arm and shoulders: _____

_____

6. Name 2 muscles in the calf area: _____

FACIAL NERVE PATTERNS

Describe what each cranial nerve is responsible for:

1. Cranial Nerve VII: _____

2. Cranial Nerve V: _____

_____

3. What is Bell's palsy?

_____

_____

4. Fill in the missing words within this paragraph using the words from the word bank below.

Cranial	Motor
Brain	Head
Spinal nerves	12
Information	Muscle nerves
Upper neck	

The _____ nerves consist of _____ pairs of nerves, one for each side of the body, that arise from the bottom of the _____ and branch out to serve the _____ and _____ area. Some of these nerves bring _____ from senses to the brain _____, some control muscles _____, and others affect glands and internal organs. _____ arise at points along the spinal canal and control sensory and _____ input from the neck down.

5. Fill in the missing words within this paragraph using the words from the word bank below.

Conjuctiva	Motor
Maxillary	Aestheticians
Mandibular	Opthalmic
Trigeminal	Innervate

Cranial nerve V is called the _____ nerve. This nerve, too, is important to us as _____ and cosmetic nurses because it is intimately associated with the face. The cranial nerve V is called the trigeminal nerve because it has three major branches; (1) the _____ nerve, (2) the _____ nerve, and (3) the _____ nerve.

The ophthalmic goes to the eye, the maxillary to the upper jaw, and a mandibular to the lower jaw. All of these branches are sensory nerves, carrying the perceptions of touch and feeling to the areas they _____ The trigeminal nerve innervates the cheek, side of the face, _____ skin of lower eyelid, side of nose. nasal vestibule, teeth tympanic membrane, and anterior two-thirds of the tongue. The _____ root of the trigeminal nerve is smaller, extending to innervate muscle in the lower jaw and floor of the mouth.

Find the key terms from the chapter within the word search using the definitions on the following page.

```
S  Y  V  G  E  T  R  P  Z  Q  N  H  A  M  S  T  R  I  N  G
L  I  I  H  A  V  U  H  K  U  A  J  T  H  K  W  W  N  W  V
W  M  P  V  W  I  V  I  P  U  B  N  H  L  E  N  J  S  A  S
I  D  X  T  U  C  H  V  I  J  O  H  U  L  O  B  C  V  H  F
F  S  R  R  F  Z  A  C  Z  I  I  W  B  I  C  Y  D  Z  E  K
H  X  V  L  Z  S  U  P  T  B  Y  P  T  A  A  N  K  X  K  H
I  F  E  N  T  E  W  C  Y  N  G  A  U  P  R  G  C  Y  P  V
Y  D  V  H  F  N  U  P  F  L  X  K  P  O  D  W  Y  O  F  W
E  I  B  Z  W  D  E  M  A  E  V  B  M  N  I  N  Y  C  W  A
M  E  H  H  D  S  M  X  L  A  M  A  D  E  A  V  H  F  E  P
T  K  P  A  W  H  U  F  E  J  L  P  T  U  C  W  C  A  U  W
U  M  J  S  Z  P  W  C  Z  A  B  A  X  R  T  Q  S  U  T  N
C  B  F  F  T  U  G  Z  B  A  R  Y  T  O  F  D  X  K  O  C
C  K  N  T  W  I  F  X  F  R  V  Q  W  S  E  X  M  T  I  X
S  F  G  Q  U  P  P  K  S  N  U  E  K  I  B  V  Y  H  U  R
W  F  L  S  O  A  F  V  J  S  B  Z  T  S  C  A  P  U  L  A
P  J  Z  B  A  L  A  Q  W  R  E  W  I  Z  Z  K  U  Z  S  A
N  N  K  D  H  Q  W  D  I  B  B  X  M  Q  Q  H  I  I  B  O
L  I  H  H  A  E  R  Q  K  E  N  D  O  M  Y  S  I  U  M  W
X  O  A  J  Q  N  B  R  A  C  H  I  A  L  I  S  C  J  N  X
```

1. It is located on the top or posterior side of the thigh area muscle group. _____

2. Upward movement _____

3. Any of the deep and thick facia, resembling flattened tendons that attach muscles to bones _____

4. Flaring cartilaginous expansion on the side of each nare ____

5. The collar bone and the humerus _____

6. Muscle cells in the heart _____

7. Important muscle for arm's ability to flex at the elbow _____

8. Side to side movement _____

9. Individual muscle fibers are protected by connective tissue _____

6 ANATOMY AND PHYSIOLOGY: THE CARDIOVASCULAR AND LYMPHATIC SYSTEMS

Date: _____

Rating: _____

Text Pages: 121–136

THE CARDIOVASCULAR SYSTEM

Solve the clues on the following page. Then look for the answer words in the puzzle below.

```
X  G  I  M  C  D  I  A  S  T  O  L  E  B  A  V  Z  Y  Q  Y
E  T  L  Y  X  K  U  N  A  J  R  E  M  R  M  N  Y  N  G  S
F  Y  W  O  S  H  K  F  J  Q  B  P  J  O  D  X  S  X  T  Y
E  L  E  C  T  R  O  L  Y  T  E  S  T  F  B  Z  K  J  X  S
G  O  Y  A  A  O  X  U  S  T  S  H  Q  G  T  G  Y  L  J  T
L  U  J  R  W  A  W  R  O  L  W  H  T  R  A  M  N  B  A  O
I  Z  A  D  H  T  P  A  I  W  B  C  N  A  R  V  Y  U  K  L
C  C  I  I  P  L  M  H  N  K  X  Y  E  N  L  L  X  Q  B  E
P  Q  O  U  E  C  P  P  W  E  E  J  X  U  P  Q  L  Z  P  Z
I  Q  H  M  W  O  V  N  U  H  E  E  M  L  A  Z  X  R  G  R
C  C  T  R  N  T  H  G  M  M  C  W  R  O  J  U  V  M  T  L
H  X  H  I  G  X  B  Q  S  U  M  C  L  C  J  K  O  I  A  F
Q  C  S  N  U  L  G  Q  F  F  X  R  Z  Y  T  F  V  H  B  B
U  O  R  P  K  C  A  U  U  O  Q  H  A  T  F  F  K  V  G  M
E  Z  X  W  A  G  V  A  R  I  C  O  S  E  V  E  I  N  G  L
Z  B  Z  S  E  L  E  K  V  Y  A  E  F  S  C  U  K  Q  X  O
S  P  H  A  G  O  C  Y  T  E  E  V  H  Y  P  O  X  I  A  Q
O  P  C  L  T  V  F  O  X  G  N  C  P  K  N  M  L  A  F  I
N  M  E  M  H  L  F  A  N  T  I  B  O  D  I  E  S  F  P  E
T  Q  B  F  O  I  T  U  L  K  B  L  Q  U  O  D  T  R  F  V
```

1.   Relaxation of the heart _____

2.   Proteins that identify and neutralize foreign bodies _____

3.   Anti-parasitic phagocytes _____

4.   A cell that has grains in it _____

5.   Decrease in oxygen in the cell _____

6.   Contraction of the heart _____

7.   A powerful immune cell _____

8.   Vein that has bulged _____

9.   Muscle tissue that "pumps" the heart _____

10. Is found in blood plasma _____

FACTS ABOUT BLOOD

Fill in the missing word.

1.   Blood is considered to have solid, liquid, and _____ properties.

2.   Our bodies produce 17 million _____ blood cells per second to replace the ones destroyed.

3.   Your body has _____ quarts of blood.

4.   The weight of our complete blood supply is roughly _____ of the total body weight.

5.   _____ blood is a brighter and more pure red compared to the duller deoxygenated load carried by the veins.

6.   Blood temperature is maintained at _____ degrees.

BLOOD COMPOSITION

Circle the best answer.

1.   The liquid component of blood is:
     a.   erythrocytes   b.   albumin
     c.   plasma   d.   hormones

2. Erythrocytes are also known as:
   a. hemoglobin
   b. white blood cells
   c. red blood cells
   d. hormones

3. Leukocytes are also known as:
   a. hemoglobin
   b. white blood cells
   c. red blood cells
   d. hormones

4. The cells that multiply at times of acute infection are:
   a. basophils
   b. hormones
   c. eosinophils
   d. neutrophils

5. The cells that provide histamine at inflammatory sites:
   a. basophils
   b. hormones
   c. eosinophils
   d. neutrophils

BLOOD DISORDERS

Write a description for each of the following terms.

1. Anemia: _____

2. Thalassemia: _____

3. Hemophilia: _____

4. Leukemia: _____

Choose the correct word from the bank of the words to match the definition.

agranulocytes   hemophilia
arterioles   phagocytes
clotting factors   thallassemia
dessication   tricuspid valve
electrolytes   varicose veins

1. _____ Smallest component of the arteries, which connect with capillary beds

2. _____ Condition characterized by swollen veins, most commonly in the legs

3. _____ Ions required by cells to regulate the electric charge and flow of water molecules across the cell membrane

4. _____ Heart valve that prevents backflow

5. _____ Disorder characterized by deficiencies of clotting factors, reducing the blood's ability to clot

6. _____ Nongranular white blood cells

7. _____ Waste-clearing white blood cells

8. _____ Specific proteins that act together in clotting; defects in specific protein changes result in clotting conditions such as hemophilia.

9. _____ Removal of all fluids

10. _____ Condition characterized by defective hemoglobin cells, resulting in oxygen deficiency

THE HEART

Answer the following questions.

1. The exterior of the heart is called the _____.

2. The heart is attached to the surrounding organs by the _____.

3. The muscle that makes the heart pump is called the _____.

4. The top two chambers of the heart are called _____.

5. The bottom two chambers of the heart are called: _____.

6. Circulation that goes from the heart to the lungs and then back again is called

_____.

7. Circulation that flows through the entire body is called _____.

HEART DISEASE

Fill in this chart by matching the correct name of a condition to its definition. Choose from the following list.

aortic aneurism
arrythmia
cardiomyopathy
congenital heart conditions
coronary artery disease
heart failure
heart valve disease
pericarditis

	Plaque caused by fat clogs the arteries, restricting oxygen and nutrients needed by the heart; often results in a heart attack
	Inflammation of the pericardium
	Reduction in the pumping ability of the heart, resulting in limited flow
	Heart rate either lower than normal or higher than normal
	Weakened pocket of lining in the aorta
	Gradual enlarging of heart tissues, resulting in heart failure
	A defect in one of the heart's structures, which occurs prior to birth
	Inefficacy of valves in the heart, resulting in backflow or limited flow

THE LYMPHATIC SYSTEM

Answer the following questions.

1. Write a description of the lymphatic system and its purpose. _____

    _____

2. Label the following on the illustration below.

    lymph capillaries
    lymph duct
    lymph nodes

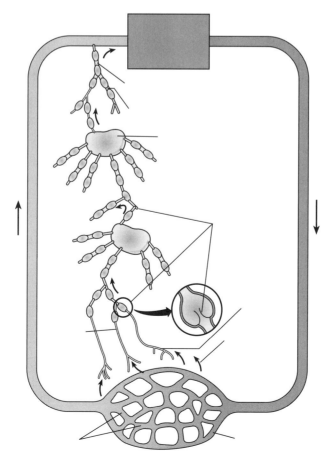

3. Without _____ and organs, fluid would accumulate, resulting in swelling and redness, a condition referred to as _____.

4. When lymph stays stagnant for any reason, a good alternative to natural lymph flow would be _____

5. _____ was the first to employ manual lymphatic drainage.

6. The benefits of lymphatic drainage are:

    a. _____

    b. _____

    c. _____

    d. _____

    e. _____

    f. _____

7 CHEMISTRY AND BIOCHEMISTRY

Date: _____

Rating: _____

Text Pages: 137–154

PRINCIPLES OF CHEMISTRY

Answer the following questions.

1. Describe the study of chemistry. _____

    _____

2. Describe matter. _____

3. Give examples of elements. _____

4. What is the smallest measurable unit of an element? _____

5. What is the nucleus of an atom made of? _____

6. Do electrons have a positive or negative charge? _____

PERIODIC TABLE OF THE ELEMENTS

Match the element to its symbol.

hydrogen _____   Cl

oxygen _____   C

carbon _____   O

sodium _____   H

chlorine _____   Na

Describe each element:

Hydrogen: _____

Oxygen: _____

_____

Carbon: _____

_____

Sodium: _____

_____

Chlorine: _____

CHEMICALS FOUND IN THE SKIN AND BODY

1. What is protein made of? _____

2. What is the basic unit of a protein molecule called? _____

3. What is the bond between amino acid groups called? _____

4. What is the name for a long chain of amino acids? _____

5. What is a simple unit of a carbohydrate called? _____

pH, ACIDS, AND BASES

Below, indicate whether each item is an acid or a base.

Cleanser _____

Toner _____

AHA _____

Bar soap _____

Skin _____

BHA _____

CHEMICAL TERMS ESTHETICIANS SHOULD KNOW

Define each term.

1. Proteo: _____

2. Lipo: _____

3. Saccharides: _____

4. Saturated: _____

_____

_____

5. Aqueous: _____

6. Aerobic: _____

_____

7. Hydration: _____

8. Homogenous: _____

9. Suspension: _____

_____

_____

10. Alcohol: _____

_____

11. Amino: _____

_____

12. Mono: _____

13. Di: _____

14. Carbo: _____

15. Distilled: _____

_____

_____

_____

16. Enzyme: _____

17. Ionized: _____

_____

18. Poly: _____

19. Tri: _____

20. Cyclo: _____

21. Aldehyde: _____

_____

BOTANICAL CHEMISTRY

Fill in the missing word.

1. Metabolites are the products used by _____ organisms in the process of metabolism.

2. Primary metabolites are so named because they are required for _____, structure, and reproduction of the plant.

3. Secondary metabolites are the products generated within the plant that are not required for the most basic, _____ sustaining needs.

4. Amino acids are _____ metabolic compounds that are naturally present in the skin.

5. Polysaccharides are made up of a large number of _____ containing monosaccharide units.

6. Alkaloids have _____ effects on the human body.

7. Carotenoids and _____ are found in deeply colored purple and blue berries, green tea, chocolate, and red vegetables.

8. _____ occurs when oxygen reacts at the unsaturated sites, causing a decomposition of the oil and the disagreeable odor associated with it.

9. An _____ is a compound structure that is formed through the reaction of an acid with an alcohol.

ESSENTIAL OIL CHEMISTRY

Use the clues to unscramble each word.

1. pentredio copunmosd   _____   Lipids made up of isoprene units

2. zeenben grin   _____   Responsible for some of the strongest antibacterial and antimicrobial compounds

3. enincfraknse   _____   Essential oil that has antiviral qualities

4. ngrmea amocilmeh   _____   Essential oil that has anti-inflammatory qualities

5. ravledne   _____   Essential oil that is a sedative

6. sslegrmaon   _____   Essential oil that has antiseptic qualities

7. maotbegr   _____   Essential oil that has anti-spasmodic qualities

8. teuplycaus   _____   Essential oil that is an expectorant

9. ymeht   _____   Essential oil that has anti-parasitic qualities

10. labsi   _____   Essential oil that helps a digestive imbalance

8 LASER, LIGHT ENERGY, AND RADIOFREQUENCY THERAPY

Date: _____

Rating: _____

Text Pages: 155-185

THE HISTORY OF LIGHT AND ENERGY DEVICES

Answer the following questions.

1. What does the acronym LASER stand for? _____

   _____

2. On the lines below, write the word that each definition describes.

   a. Small particles of energy _____

   b. The measurement from the distance of the top of one wave to top of the next

      _____

   c. A billionth of a meter _____

   d. Made up of a multitude of visible and invisible infrared wavelength of light _____

      _____

   e. All laser light traveling in the same direction _____

   f. Laser light made up of 1 wavelength and 1 color _____

   g. Attraction of a particular wavelength of light toward a specific target _____

   h. What vascular lasers seek out _____

   i. Destruction of a target using thermal energy _____

   j. The time necessary for a chromophore, blood vessel, or hair follicle to lose the majority
      of heat by diffusion _____

PHYSICS

Write in the definition for each of the following words.

1. Power density: _____
   _____

2. Fluence: _____
   _____

3. Pulse duration or pulse width: _____
   _____
   _____

4. Spot size: _____
   _____

5. List five items contained in the ANSI Z136.3 document. _____
   _____
   _____

6. What does LSO stand for? _____

7. List five items the LSO is responsible for:
   _____
   _____
   _____
   _____
   _____
   _____

LASER CLASSIFICATIONS

Answer the following questions.

1. How is the system used to classify lasers different than the FDA classification of medical devices?
   _____
   _____

2. Write the class number (1, 2, 3, or 4) next to each description.

   _____ Do not pose any hazard under normal viewing conditions.

_____ Common examples are compact disc players or laser printers.

_____ CO_2 and Erbium

_____ Examples include laser pointers and IPL devices.

_____ These devices are potentially hazardous if viewed directly.

_____ These devices are exempt from labeling requirements.

_____ The range is 400 nanometers (nm) to 700 nanometers (nm).

_____ These devices are the most hazardous of all laser systems.

_____ These lasers include ophthalmic eye lasers.

LASER SAFETY

Answer the following questions.

1. What is ocular protection?

   _____

2. How can you control airborne contaminants?

   _____

3. What type of filter is most recommended for controlling airborne contaminants?

   _____

4. How do you prevent the possibility of fire and explosion?

   _____

   _____

   _____

5. In Table 8-1, the Laser, RF, and IPL Safety Policy and Procedure, who does it say should be responsible for selecting the appropriate delivery system?

   _____

LASER THERAPY

Answer the following questions.

1. Explain a Photothermal Tissue Reaction:

   _____

   _____

_____
_____
_____

2. Explain how a vascular laser works.

_____
_____
_____
_____
_____
_____

LASER THERAPY

Fill in the blanks using words from the word bank.

532 nm to 1,064 nm	micro thermal zones
darkening	photomechanical
deeper	pigmented
fractional resurfacing	Q-switched laser
lentigo	water

1. Noting the absorption spectrum of oxyhemoglobin coupled with the depth of epidermal and dermal vessels, lasers ranging from _____ are the most appropriate for vascular lesions.

2. Remember, the longer the wavelength, the _____ the penetration.

3. Photothermal nonablative devices can also be used very successfully for the treatment of _____ lesions.

4. The immediate response of skin experiencing photothermal lasers is either _____, which occurs with melanin break-up, or erythema due to local inflammation.

5. Within 24 hours after the treatment, one can see a crusting or darkening over the _____ or age spot; melanin absorbs the light, which is transformed to heat.

6. Recently, there has been an explosion of new technology in the field of _____ _____.

7. In 2004, Reliant Technologies developed the Fraxel laser, a 1,550-nm wavelength that is absorbed by _____ but cannot be delivered microscopically in a pixel-type matrix. These columns of thermal energy are called _____.

8. The _____ is the best laser for exploding particles of tattoo ink.

9. The type of laser in question 8 is known as a _____ laser.

10. Draw a line matching the name of the laser to its wavelength.

Q-switched for black pigment	694 nm
Q-switched (alexandrite)	800 nm
diode for endovenous fibers	755 nm
ruby for hair removal	980 nm
diode for hair removal	694 nm
Nd:YAG	1,550 nm
Fraxel YAG	1,064 nm

INTENSE PULSED LIGHT

Fill in the blanks from the word bank below.

1995	filter
broad spectrum	hair shaft
chromophore	photodamaged

1. The first IPL emerged in _____

2. With the variety of skin chromophores, it makes sense to use a broadband light to treat the variety of skin abnormalities seen with _____ skin.

3. Lasers treat one _____ with one monochromatic light while intense pulsed light can target multiple chromophores.

4. The IPL device consists of a flashlamp housed in a treatment head with _____ systems that can select a specific spectrum of visible and invisible wavelengths.

5. A _____ filter spans from 500 nm to 1,400 nm.

6. The _____ will require a longer wavelength such as a red filter.

7. Give definitions for the following terms:

   a. Pulsed (1 to 3 pulses): _____

   _____

   _____

   _____

_____

b. Skin cooling: _____

_____

_____

_____

_____

_____

c. IPL with radio frequency: _____

_____

_____

_____

d. Variable pulse duration: _____

_____

e. Variable fluence: _____

_____

f. Large vs. small spot size: _____

_____

_____

g. Variable inter-pulse delay: _____

_____

_____

_____

RADIOFREQUENCY DEVICES

Answer the following questions.

1. What is a monopolar RF device used for in surgery centers?

_____

2. What does impedance mean?

_____

3. What is another name for a dispersing electrode?

_____

4. What was the first nonablative monopolar device used for?

_____

5. What is used for skin cooling?

_____

6. Explain a bipolar radiofrequency energy:

_____

_____

_____

LIGHT-EMITTING DIODES (LED DEVICES) AND LOW-LEVEL LIGHT THERAPY

Answer the following questions.

1. What is photomodulation?

_____

_____

2. What are cytochromes?

_____

3. What is the most common LED color wavelength?

_____

4. What else is LED therapy being clinically used for?

a. _____

b. _____

c. _____

d. _____

5. What benefits does a low-level laser light have for a client?

_____

6. What benefits are offered by LED rejuvenation?

a. _____

b. _____

c. _____

d. _____

e. _____

f. _____

g. _____

7. Fill in the crossword using the clues below.

Across

5. Acronym for Intense Pulse Light
7. Pink, sometimes scaly, abnormal skin lesions that are regarded to be pre-cancerous. (2 words)
8. Parallel rays of light that are traveling spatially and temporally in phase with each other. (2 words)

Down

1. Irradiance multiplied by the exposure time, measured in joules.
2. Capable of ablation
3. Metric measurement indicating a billionth of a meter.
4. Protection factor provided by a filter material at a specific wavelength of laser light.

10. A measurement of a unit of energy from a pulsed laser or light source.

6. It is the part of a molecule responsible for its color.

9. Acronym for Light Amplification of the Stimulated Emission of Radiation.

9 NUTRITION AND STRESS MANAGEMENT

Date: _____

Rating: _____

Text Pages: 187–199

NUTRIENTS AND DIET

Answer the following questions.

1. What are the components of food? _____

2. What are the two processes in metabolism? _____

3. The building up of tissue happens during which process? _____

4. The breaking down of tissue happens during which process? _____

THE ESTHETIC BENEFITS OF VITAMINS

Draw a line from the vitamin to its description.

Vitamin A   Helps accelerate hair growth

Vitamin B1   Essential for maintaining natural skin color

Vitamin B2   Also known as riboflavin

Vitamin B3   Helps hair, skin, and nails stay supple

Vitamin B5   Helps control the flow of oil from sebaceous glands

Vitamin B6   Essential in the formation of collagen protein

Vitamin B7   Also known as cobalamin

Vitamin B9   Improves skin ability to take in oxygen

Vitamin B12   Protects against sun damage

Vitamin C   Also known as folic acid

Vitamin D   Slows down skin aging

Vitamin E   Greatly aids in skin respiration

FREE RADICALS AND ANTIOXIDANTS

Answer the following questions.

1. How are free radicals created?

    _____

2. Describe an antioxidant.

    _____

    _____

3. How does an antioxidant neutralize a free radical?

    _____

4. What foods can antioxidants be found in?

    _____

5. Why is acne sometimes an indicator of poor nutrition?

    _____

    _____

6. Which foods can create sluggishness and lead to weight gain? _____

    _____

7. Which foods can deplete B vitamins, resulting in anxiety, fatigue, headaches, and irritability? _____

NUTRITION AND AGING

Answer the following questions.

1. Describe glycation.

    _____

    _____

    _____

    _____

2. Which diseases does glycation contribute to?

_____

_____

3. Which foods contain the highest concentration of AGE products?

_____

_____

_____

SMOKING AND THE SKIN

Answer the following questions.

1. How many years can skin be aged prematurely by smoking? _____

2. Tobacco smoke contains thousands of _____.

3. What affect does smoking have on the capillaries in the face? _____

_____

4. Smokers are at a higher risk for which ailments? _____

_____

WHAT WE CAN DO TO SLOW THESE PROCESSES

Answer the following questions.

1. To slow the aging process, cooking temperatures should be kept under

_____.

2. Supplements that look promising to help fight AGE are _____

_____.

3. List seven foods that have low concentrations of Advanced Glycation Endproducts:

_____

_____

EFFECTS OF STRESS ON THE BODY

Explain why the following effects happen.

1. Dullness: _____

2. Congestion: _____
    _____

3. Breakouts: _____
    _____

4. Sensitivities and/or irritation: _____
    _____
    _____
    _____

STRESS MANAGEMENT

Explain why it would be beneficial to accomplish the following.

1. Breathing: _____
    _____
    _____

2. Put on the brakes: _____
    _____
    _____

3. Practice anger control: _____
    _____

4. Go for a walk: _____
    _____
    _____

5. Solve the clues below. Then look for the answer words in the following puzzle.

```
C Q L A Z C G O H Q Z A G Z T R B B O N
P D L F P P J O V C F Z L M T W P G Q G
Z I E V O O C N D I X W Y N Y X S E O V
P R X M F L S F G F D R C J I Y C K U D
M N M E G E I V M Q A Q A Z D L Z E P Z
Y N D T N U S C W T G Q T J Y R J W A U
W P W A Q U F C A P E N I V F C B S R H
B H K B J C I A A C A A O J Z O Q O W P
I J I O Q A X L P T I M N J R R W P H U
W K N L A K X R X A A D L R U T M U W Z
I S I I S S L Y C D N B A Q I I Z B N Q
X K A S A D G I G U V M O Z Y S Z T S Q
I A C M Y U H B M E L R R L E O O M Q G
T N I K S Z S Z P Q L F Y Q I L D S T B
V O N V M O S O S A J F L G R S E B R X
I E N T J U N N C N L Z B I Z J M N V E
W S K R Y R Q X E H Q W P R E Z H M U S
V H M Z U S S D O C Q I R A D I C A L W
V U C R A Y A I Y T E R K J N U L H P N
F A I H X O L J Z P P N A F U X L D N F
```

1. Breaks down large units of living matter _____

2. A destructive biological process _____

3. Advanced Glycation Endproducts _____

4. A hormone released by the adrenal gland _____

5. Unbalanced oxygen molecule: free _____

6. Process of changing food into forms it can use to provide energy _____

7. Also known as Vitamin B3 _____

8. Also known as Vitamin B9 _____

10 ADVANCED SKIN DISORDERS: SKIN IN DISTRESS

Date: _____

Rating: _____

Text Pages: 200–234

THE INFLAMMATION CASCADE

Answer the following questions.

1. What happens when a cell gets irritated? _____
   _____

2. The immune system then sends leukocytes, or white blood cells, to the site of irritation, and the leukocytes release another special chemical called a _____

3. There are different stages of wounds. A compromised epidermis would be a _____
   _____

4. An example of a Stage 2 wound is a second-degree _____

5. How quickly does a superficial wound heal? _____

6. What word means control of bleeding? _____

7. The final phase of wound healing is characterized by an increase in strength without an increase in collagen content; this is called the _____

WOUND REPAIR

Answer the following questions.

1. Describe a simple suture: _____
   _____

2. Describe a buried suture: _____
   _____

3. Describe a running suture: _____
   _____
   _____

4. What is applied to protect the wound from contaminants, reduce pain, and absorb exudates as the wound heals? _____

5. What should people who smoke be aware of? _____

_____

_____

6. What effect can the sun have on a wound? _____

SUN DAMAGE

Write T next to the true statements and F next to the false statements.

_____   There is no such thing as short-term sun damage.

_____   Reddening of the skin is an example of short-term sun damage.

_____   Sunburn skin will eventually peel due to the extreme dryness.

_____   Sunburn is a non-medical condition.

_____   Treatments for sunburn include cool packs, a cool bath with vinegar added to water, an application of plain yogurt to the area, or the use of over-the-counter anesthetic sprays if the client is not allergic to them.

_____   Many sunburns occur when people are out of their normal environment or are ignorant about sun protection.

_____   You cannot get hyperpigmentation from the sun.

_____   Sun-induced skin discoloration begins in the late teens and early 20s and gets continually worse.

_____   Chloasma (liver spots) are caused by long-term sun exposure.

_____   Tinea versicolor is what many refer to as sun spots or sun fungus.

_____   Tinea versicolor is characterized by brown spots on the skin.

Answer the following questions.

1. How does sun exposure create free radicals? _____

_____

_____

_____

2. Which cells get chased away by sun exposure? _____

3. What percentage of sun damage do we receive in childhood and adolescence? _____

4. List some of the effects of the sun on the skin: _____

_____

_____

5. Define dermatoheliosis. _____

6. What effect does the sun have on the dermis? _____

_____

SKIN CANCERS AND OTHER SUN-RELATED SKIN GROWTHS

Unscramble the following terms using the definitions as clues.

1. atincic skeartois   _____   Rough areas of sun-damaged skin indicated by dysplastic cell growth

2. pldysatcis   _____   Abnormal growth

3. thrcyrpyaeo   _____   Freezing with liquid nitrogen

4. ebascuoes ayprheaplis   _____   Small, donut-shaped lesions that look like large, open comedones surrounded by a ridge of skin

5. csebrroihe sekiarots   _____   Large, flat, crusty-looking, brown, black, yellowish, or gray lesions often found on the faces of older, sun-damaged clients

6. gilenitnes   _____   Also known as solar freckles

7. kisn ancerc   _____   Condition caused by cells dividing unevenly and rapidly but the genetic material in the DNA has been damaged from the sun.

8. Describe how a spot of basal cell carcinoma appears: _____

_____

_____

9. Describe how a spot of squamous cell carcinoma appears: _____

_____

_____

10. Describe how a spot of melanoma appears: _____

_____

11. What are the ABCDEs of melanoma?

A: _____

B: _____

C: _____
_____

D: _____
_____

E: _____
_____

12. Name the various cancers in the following pictures:

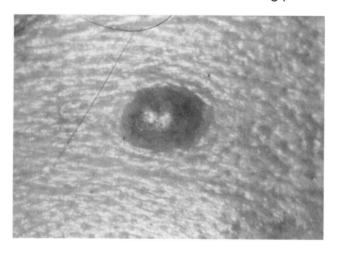

_____

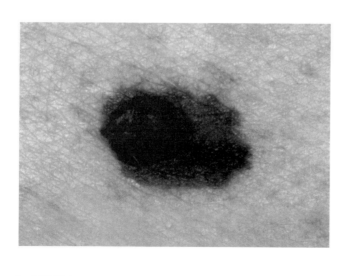

_____

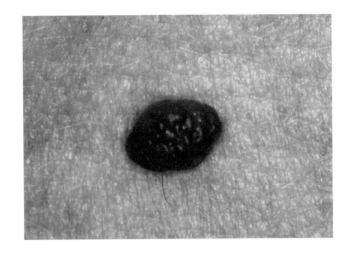

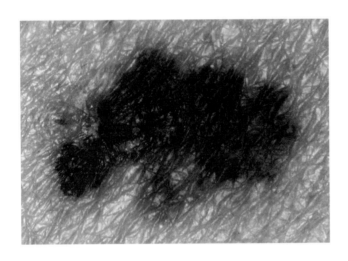

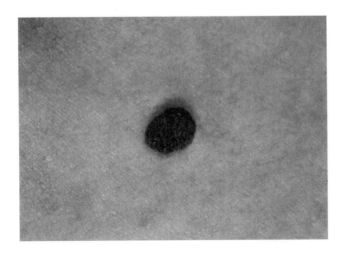

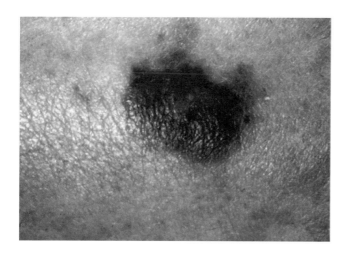

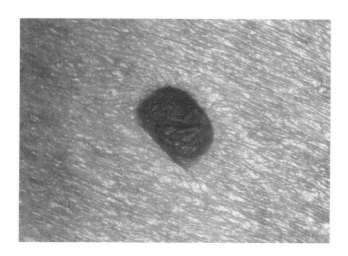

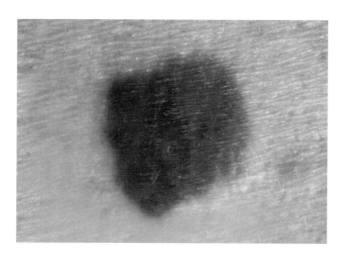

ACNE

Use the words from the word bank to answer the following questions.

acne vulgaris   ostium
closed comedones   papule
lamellar granules   *Propionibacterium acnes*
microcomedones   pustule
nodule   retention hyperkeratosis
non-inflammatory

1. Acne is a distressed skin condition that results in inflammatory and _____ lesions.

2. The most common form of acne is called _____.

3. The hereditary condition in which cells are retained is called _____.

4. Some researchers believe that retention hyperkeratosis is caused by an inability of the body to produce intercellular structures called _____.

5. _____ are a mixture of dead cell buildup, bacteria, fatty acids from the sebum, and other cellular debris.

6. The opening of the follicle is called the _____.

7. The bacteria that causes acne vulgaris is _____.

8. Small "underground" bumps that are not easily extracted are called _____.

9. A _____ is a red, sore bump without a "whitehead."

10. A _____ is closer to the skin's surface and dilates the follicle opening, relieving the pressure on the nerve endings resulting in less pain.

11. A _____ is similar to a papule, but it is deeper in the skin and feels very solid and sore.

12. Describe each grade of acne:

    a. Grade 1 acne: _____

        _____

    b. Grade 2 acne: _____

        _____

c. Grade 3 acne: _____

_____

_____

d. Grade 4 acne: _____

_____

HORMONES

Answer the following questions.

1. Testosterone, an androgen, converts to _____ DHT, another form of male hormone, which "switches on" the oil gland.

2. Premenstrual acne flare-ups are caused by the _____ hormone.

3. A sudden flow of sebum in the follicle causes _____

4. Women that get acne on their chins can be treated with _____ treatments.

5. What are some of the causes of acne breakouts in women? _____

_____

ACNE AND ROSACEA

Answer the following questions.

1. Explain what keratosis pilaris is. _____

_____

2. Sun exposure may temporarily dry up acne, but it does cause _____, which can add to or increase the chances of acne flare-ups.

3. How does overcleaning the skin affect acne? _____

_____

_____

4. Describe self-trauma excoriations: _____

_____

5. Write T next to the true statements and F next to the false statements.

_____ Greasy foods can add to breakouts.

_____ Milk and some milk products have been found to cause acne problems.

_____ Some cosmetics can contribute to acne.

_____ Seborrheic dermatitis is characterized by really oily skin.

_____ Seborrheic dermatitis may be associated with a yeast called pityrosporum ovale.

_____ Perioral dermatitis is dermatitis around the mouth.

_____ Rosacea is characterized by oily skin only.

_____ Clients with rosacea have some flushing and some telangiectases.

_____ Rosacea is a vascular disorder.

_____ The sudden flushing of blood to the face triggers the release of a biochemical within the skin called vascular growth factor.

6. List and describe the following types of rosacea:

a. Erythematotelangiectatic rosacea: _____

_____

b. Papulopustular rosacea: _____

_____

c. Phymatous rosacea: _____

_____

SKIN TYPING AND AGING ANALYSIS

Date: _____

Rating: _____

Text Pages: 235–248

FITZPATRICK SKIN TYPING SCALE

1. Fill in the blank cells in the following chart.

Skin Type	Skin Color	Hair and Eye Color	Reaction to Sun	Common Ethnic Considerations
Type I		Blond hair and		English,
Type II	White			Northern European
Type III				
Type IV	Brown	Brown hair and		
Type V				Asian, Indian, some Africans
Type VI	Black		Tans, never burns, deeply pigmented, never freckles	

2. Answer the following questions to determine your Fitzpatrick type.

Points

Question	0	1	2	3	4	Score
What color are your eyes?	Light blue, gray, green	Blue, gray or green	Blue	Dark brown	Brownish black	

Points

Question	0	1	2	3	4	Score
What is the natural color of your hair?	Sandy red	Blond	Chestnut/ dark blond	Dark brown	black	
What color is your skin (unexposed areas)?	Reddish	Very pale	Pale with beige tint	Light brown	Dark brown	
Do you have freckles on unexposed areas?	Many	Several	Few	Incidental	None	
Genetic Disposition Total						

Points

Question	0	1	2	3	4	Score
What happens when you stay too long in the sun?	Painful, redness, blistering, peeling	Blistering followed by peeling	Burns sometimes followed by peeling	Rare burns	Never had burns	
To what degree do you turn brown?	Hardly or not at all	Light color tan	Reasonable tan	Tan very easily	Turn dark brown quickly	
Do you turn brown with several hours of sun exposure?	Never	Seldom	Sometimes	Often	Always	
How does your face react to the sun?	Very sensitive	Sensitive	Normal	Very resistant	Never had a problem	
Reaction to Sun Exposure Total						

Questions	Points					Score
	0	1	2	3	4	
When did you last expose your body to sun (or artificial sunlamp/ tanning cream)?	More than 3 months ago	2–3 months ago	1–2 months ago	Less than a month ago	Less than 2 weeks ago	
Did you expose the area to be treated to the sun?	Never	Hardly ever	Sometimes	Often	Always	
Tanning Habits Total						

Add all three scores together for a total score: _____ + _____ + _____ = _____

If your score is between 0 and 7, you are a Fitzpatrick I.

If your score is between 8 and 16, you are a Fitzpatrick II.

If your score is between 17 and 25, you are a Fitzpatrick III.

If your score is between 26 and 30, you are a Fitzpatrick IV.

Over 30, you are a Fitzpatrick V or VI.

THE GLOGAU SCALE

Circle the best answer to each question.

1. The Glogau classification system evaluates the level of _____ based on wrinkling.

a. creasing   b. photodamage
c. hyperpigmentation   d. pigment

2. Type I on this scale is described as having _____

a. wrinkles at rest—you see the wrinkles when the person is not moving
b. no wrinkles at rest or while moving
c. wrinkles only in motion
d. wrinkles as predominant characteristic

3. Type II describes someone who has _____

a. no keratosis
b. acne scarring
c. early to moderate photoaging

4. Type IV describes someone with _____

a. mild photoaging
b. advanced photoaging
c. severe photoaging

RUBIN CLASSIFICATIONS

Answer the following questions.

1. Describe Level 1 on this scale:

_____

_____

2. Which treatments would you perform on a Rubin Level 1? _____

3. Describe Level 2:

_____

_____

_____

4. Which treatments would you perform on a Rubin Level 2?

_____

_____

5. Describe Level 3:

_____

_____

_____

6. Which treatments would you perform on a Rubin Level 3?

_____

KLIGMAN ROSACEA CLASSIFICATION

Answer the following questions.

1. How many stages of rosacea are there? _____

2. Describe Stage I: _____

_____

3. Describe Stage II: _____

_____

4. Describe Stage III: _____

_____

ORIENTAL REFLEX ZONES OF THE FACE _____

Fill in the blanks.

1. In Western schools, they teach that the body is made up not only of solids and fluids but of _____ as well.

2. The vital-energy, as it is called in Western countries, is a very subtle form of energy essential to all life forms. In China it is called _____

3. The pathways for energy flow within the body are called _____ for acupuncture and _____ for Ayurveda.

4. In traditional Chinese medicine, there are five elements. They are _____

_____

5. The element that is associated with the energies of the liver and the gallbladder is _____

6. The element that is associated with the energies of the heart and the small intestine is

_____

7. The element that is associated with the energies of the kidneys and bladder is _____

8. When one of the five elements is out of balance, undesirable conditions can be created. Name the element that is associated with these various conditions.

Oily skin, blackheads, and hyperpigmentation   _____

Dry, dull, lifeless skin   _____

Lymph circulation problems   _____

Dehydration, lack of tone, wrinkles   _____

Irritated, red, sensitive scalp   _____

REFLEX ZONES OF THE FACE

Match the zones and organs listed below with the location on the face by drawing a line to the corresponding answer.

between the eyebrows   upper lip

temple areas   spleen

bridge of nose   chin area

lower part of the circle around the eye   liver

cheeks   gallbladder

hormones   spleen

heart   lungs

ISOTYPES

Answer the following question.

Describe the difference between an estrogen isotype and androgen isotype.

_____

_____

_____

_____

_____

_____

_____

12 SKIN CARE PRODUCTS: INGREDIENTS AND CHEMISTRY

Date: _____

Rating: _____

Text Pages: 249–280

CATEGORIES OF COSMETIC INGREDIENTS

Answer the following questions.

1. What is the definition of cosmetic chemistry? _____

   _____

2. Tell how each term applies to cosmetic chemistry.

   a. Biology: _____

   _____

   b. Chemistry: _____

   _____

   c. Medicine: _____

   _____

   _____

   d. Pharmacology: _____

   _____

   _____

   e. Cosmetology: _____

   _____

   _____

3. What are the two basic categories of ingredients? _____

4. The word *drug* is defined as:_____

   _____

5. The word *cosmetics* is defined as: _____

_____

_____

6. What is a drug claim? _____

_____

7. Define cosmeceuticals: _____

_____

_____

8. What is a vehicle? _____

9. What is deionized water used for? _____

EMOLLIENTS

1. Unscramble each word using the definition as a clue.

a.	teproactnst	_____	Ingredients that keep water from evaporating
b.	nemrlai loi	_____	An example of a protectant
c.	ermutaplot	_____	Commonly known as petroleum jelly
d.	eciilsno	_____	State-of-the-art chemical groups used in skin care
e.	eomthiidecn	_____	A common form of silicone
f.	rsspigne tganes	_____	Helps blushes and powders stay in cake form
g.	lgbociiyolal irtne	_____	Describes substances that will not cross-react with natural skin functioning reactions

Answer the following questions.

2. Define *comedogenicity*. _____

_____

3. Define *retention hyperkeratosis*. _____

4. Look for the following emollients in the word search puzzle on the next page.

castor (oil)   rice bran (oil)
coconut (oil)   safflower (oil)
grapeseed (oil)   soybean (oil)
jojoba (oil)   sunflower (oil)
palm (oil)

```
K A W D I X V D Z T U Z S L U I G Q X D
Q M V Y M H R A M O S A G M B Y B R E S
W T S N V P X E T N A V J F X X A E O N
Z F G K K Y P Z N N J A O J Q B S B Q O
S H D W A P S V J S C E H M O E Z L Y D
T U A T E F W Q O A E A K J P Z I Y U Y
E U N B O J S E K F M L O A V G V E F L
C M G F X X V P U F Z J R Y F E M Z P G
O G G I L C Q A F L G G C A S T O R R P
C L S R B O E L F O O W Z Y V M Y X A O
O E I Y M B W M E W G U Y J Y G M U N S
N A V X F J U E N E C C L V E O W P K Y
U Y R W P I L N R R P O O G X J Y S D A
T T Q H N O U F X X H W I O V B W B Q E
N V I X H V G X Q L B L K K K J D L O J
M F L P F K Z S U N F L O N E R I C Z T
O U Q Y R Q I Y X J F U E S G I U O C X
S W Z J G Z Z Z E X E Q X Q C D W N D U
M P P E X C U J K V S W S O Y B E A N Z
X G T M R I C E B R A N E I M P I Z Y Z
```

5. List waxes derived from plant sources.

   a. _____

   b. _____

   c. _____

   d. _____

6. List waxes derived from animal sources.

   a. _____

   b. _____

7. List waxes derived from petroleum sources.

    a. _____

    b. _____

8. List other synthetic waxes.

    a. _____

    b. _____

FATTY ACIDS

Each of the following terms is described below. Match the definitions to the terms.

caprylic acid   oleic acid
lauric acid   palmitic acid
myristic acid   stearic acid

1. _____ Derived from animal fat or plant oil; frequently used in creams, including shaving cream; also used in making soap and candles

2. _____ Derived from coconut or palm seed oil, nutmeg butter, animal fat, and other vegetable fats

3. _____ The main fatty acid in coconut and palm oil; used in the manufacture of the well-known surfactant sodium lauryl sulfate

4. _____ Derived from coconut oil, palm oil, or animal fat

5. _____ Derived from palm oil or palm kernel oil, but occurs naturally in many dairy products

6. _____ Derived from animal fats and olive and grapeseed oil

FATTY ALCOHOLS

Unscramble each word using the definition as a clue.

1. auryll (alcohol) _____ Also known as dodecanol, used as an emollient and emulsifier

2. lestayr (alcohol) _____ Emollient, emulsifier, and thickener, foam booster for foaming cleansers; can be animal or plant derived

3. oeyll (alcohol)   _____   Multi-use functional ingredient used as an
                                           emollient, thickener, and emulsifier; used in
                                           superfatted soaps and has an oilier feel than
                                           other fatty alcohols

4. yltecare (alcohol)   _____   A mixture of cetyl and stearyl alcohol used as a
                                           foam booster, stabilizer, thickener, and to give a
                                           silky feel to products

SURFACTANTS

Answer the following questions.

1. List the four types of surfactants.

    a. _____

    b. _____

    c. _____

    d. _____

2. List five examples of surfactants.

    a. _____

    b. _____

    c. _____

    d. _____

    e. _____

        _____

        _____

3. What do surface active agents do? _____

    _____

4. What are the names of the two ends on a surfactant polymer molecule? _____

    _____

5. What is the name for the condition of oil or fat being evenly suspended in water? _____

    _____

6. In the condition mentioned in question 5, what are the oil or fat parts referred to? _____

7. In the condition mentioned in question 5, which would be the external phase, the oil or
    the water? _____

PHYSICAL EMULSIONS

List eight frequently used emulsifiers.

1. _____

2. _____

3. _____

4. _____

5. _____

6. _____

7. _____

8. _____

SOLVENTS

Describe the two parts to a solution.

_____

HIGH-TECH VEHICLES

Answer the following questions.

1. Describe a vehicle.

   _____

2. Describe a miscelle.

   _____

3. Describe microencapsulation.

   _____

4. Describe liposomes.

   _____

5. Describe microsponges.

   _____

ANTIMICROBIALS AND PRESERVATIVES

1. Look for the following preservatives in the word search puzzle.

butylparaben
DMDM (hydantoin)
diazolidinyl (urea)
imidazolidinyl (urea)

methylparaben
propylparaben
quaternium(-15)

```
N A W D W G M G F F I Z W Y N A F A S R
F Q F I Q M F O Y E M L G Z L V B G B R
J O D A S I P N C V I P Q Z T P T M R B
S F T Z Z L L S X H D A U Y S R Q O N S
O V S O Z Y W N E B A N K Q G O S S A D
O I L L R H G D C F Z M S Q Y P L C Z H
A D T I D R D I X X O X H W P Y A N I H
P F E D E Q B U F H L E S E D L F U Y M
S A N I O U U X A S I J O I X P T Y H E
F Z X N E A S B W W D P E J B A L Q I T
J G U Y V T H J O S I Z K G A R O V R H
Q D A L N E C H G V N O F M O A U J V Y
E A M H T R B Z J T Y F I B N B R Y R L
E W N D V N Q A B Q L R H V L E U A B P
R U N D M I T B D C W E V O T N B O O A
Z D J V B U F O V L R B Y C C T X W S R
F X N H F M I F P S D F C J C B E K W A
B U T Y L P A R A B E N Z H Q N X O Q B
O Y U Z R M D W H N R Q C P B D C J U E
U H J Y Q W K I H X Q S I E C L G P A N
```

2. Each of the following terms is described below. Match the definitions to the terms.

astringents   essential oils
buffering   gellant
chelating agent   sodium lauryl sulfate
coloring agent   sodium tallowate
colors   xantan gum

    a. A _____ is a chemical that is added to cosmetics to improve the efficiency of the preservative.

    b. _____ refers to adjusting the pH of a product to make it more acceptable to the skin.

    c. A _____ is an agent that is added to a product to give it a gel-like consistency.

    d. _____ is a natural sugar complex used as a gellant.

    e. _____ are added to make products more appealing to consumers.

    f. Iron oxide is an example of a _____

    g. In some products _____ are used for fragrance.

    h. A common detergent ingredient used in cleansers is _____

    i. A common fat that is used in bar soap is _____

    f. _____ are an example of a performance agent.

3. Unscramble each word using the definition as a clue.

    a. lauarnt ignoisurmtzi rsofatc   _____   Natural humectants, lipids, or hydrating agents found within the intercellular cement

    b. diusom ACP   _____   An example of an NMF

    c. loschterloe   _____   Another example of an NMF

    d. dipli acemnerplte   _____   Process accomplished by applying a group of lipid ingredients to the skin

    e. olelniic dica   _____   An example of the group referred to in question d

    f. opyleprne lcoygl   _____   A widely used humectant

g. lotsrobi   _____   An excellent hydrating
                                                       agent frequently used in
                                                       lotions

h. hlauryicno dcai   _____   A water binder that works
                                                       differently than standard
                                                       hydrophilic agents

i. psscchumooydlaarei   _____   Carbohydrate-lipid
                                                       complexes that are also
                                                       good water binders

j. cosievclu   _____   A heavy, large molecule that
                                                       sits on top of the skin and
                                                       prevents moisture loss

k. proelumta   _____   A good example of an
                                                       occlusive

EXFOLIANTS

Answer the following questions.

1. What does an exfoliant accomplish? _____

    _____

2. What are the two types of exfoliants? _____

3. Give four examples of mechanical exfoliants.

    a. _____

    b. _____

    c. _____

    d. _____

4. Give three examples of chemical exfoliants.

    a. _____

    b. _____

    c. _____

5. List the benefits of a glycolic acid treatment.

    a. _____

    _____

    _____

    b. _____

    _____

    _____

    _____

    _____

    c. _____

    _____

    _____

    _____

    _____

    d. _____

    _____

    _____

    _____

    _____

    _____

    e. _____

    _____

    f. _____

    _____

    _____

6. List the contraindications of alpha hydroxy acids.

    a. _____

    b. _____

    _____

    c. _____

    d. _____

    e. _____

    f. _____

    g. _____

h. _____

i. _____

j. _____

k. _____

l. _____

7.   List other exfoliants that are available.

a. _____

b. _____

c. _____

d. _____

e. _____

FREE RADICALS

Answer the following questions.

1.   What is a free radical? _____

_____

_____

_____

2.   What is the inflammation cascade? _____

_____

3.   Name three types of self-destruct enzymes. _____

4.   When sun exposure causes an oxygen molecule to split, it creates one stable and one unstable oxygen atom that has lost electrons to the stable atom. This unstable oxygen atom is a free radical and is also known as a _____

5.   Iron is one of the most reactive elements and loses electrons or _____

6.   Unscramble the following antioxidants.

nviamit C   _____

itvmnai E   _____

teab eenracot   _____

xidupsreoe mustaidse _____

rppoec _____

degaperse traextc _____

cyprinanothoadnsi _____

heppoylnosl _____

hroltocpeo _____

socracbi diac _____

gcilae acdi _____

copiil daci _____

SUNSCREEN INGREDIENTS

Define the following terms.

1. Octinoxate: _____
   _____

2. Octisalate: _____
   _____

3. Oxybenzone: _____
   _____

4. Avobenzene: _____

5. Ecamsule: _____
   _____

PEPTIDES AND COLLAGEN STIMULANTS

Answer the following questions.

1. Describe palmitoyl pentapeptide-3. _____
   _____
   _____

2. Other peptides that are found to be beneficial are _____
   _____

3. Explain glucans (also called beta glucans). _____

_____

_____

_____

4. What is TRF? _____

_____

5. Explain glycoproteins. _____

_____

_____

13 BOTANICALS AND AROMATHERAPY

Date: _____

Rating: _____

Text Pages: 281–304

WHAT ARE BOTANICAL INGREDIENTS?

Answer the following questions.

1. What role do botanical fixed oils, essential oils, herbal extracts, and other plant-based therapies have on cosmetic preparations?

   _____

2. What does *botanical* mean? _____

3. The benefits of plant extracts include:

   a. _____

   b. _____

   c. _____

   d. _____

   e. _____

   f. _____

   g. _____

   h. _____

   i. _____

4. In what skin-care applications are plant derivatives used?

   a. _____

   b. _____

   c. _____

   d. _____

e. _____

f. _____

g. _____

5. Define *whole extract*.

_____

_____

6. Define and give an example of an isolate.

_____

_____

_____

7. What is a tincture?

_____

8. How do you make an herbal infusion?

_____

_____

9. What is a fixed oil?

_____

10. Give examples of fixed oils.

_____

11. How do they get the oils out of the above natural substance?

_____

12. What is a method of extraction that is popular in the fragrance industry?

_____

BOTANICALS FOR SKIN CARE

Fill in the missing cells in the chart.

Name of Botanical	Properties	Uses
Aloe Vera	Anti-inflammatory, regenerative, moisturizing, soothing, healing	Burns,
Arnica	Anti-inflammatory	

Name of Botanical	Properties	Uses
Bamboo		
Cocoa	Anti-inflammatory, antioxidant, emollient, regenerative	General skin care and conditioning,
Comfrey		
Green Tea	Anti-inflammatory, circulatory stimulant	
Kelp	Wound healing, detoxifying	
Marigold		
Shea Butter		

AROMATHERAPY AND ESSENTIAL OILS

Answer the following questions.

1. How does a practitioner use essential oils effectively?

    _____

    _____

2. When did the practice of aromatherapy begin?

    _____

    _____

    _____

    _____

    _____

3. What are essential oils?

    _____

    _____

4. What is the olfactory system? _____

5. What is homeostasis?

   _____

   _____

6. What does the limbic system do?

   _____

7. What role does the hypothalamus play?

   _____

   _____

8. What topical applications can be achieved with essential oils?

   a. _____

   b. _____

   c. _____

   d. _____

   e. _____

   f. _____

ESSENTIAL OIL CHEMISTRY

Fill in the missing cells in the chart.

Chemical Family	Essential Oils with Influential Amounts	Properties	Cautions	Examples of Individual Components within the Family
Sesquiterpene Hydrocarbons	German chamomile,	Anti-allergic, anti-inflammatory, cooling		chamazulene beta-caryophyllene
Monoterpene Alcohols *The most beneficial and safest of the aromatic molecules*	Lavender MQV Palmarosa,			linalool borneol menthol terpinen-4-ol

STANDARD PRACTICAL WORKBOOK

Chemical Family	Essential Oils with Influential Amounts	Properties	Cautions	Examples of Individual Components within the Family
Sesquiterpene Alcohols				cedrol santalol-alpha-bisabolol
Aldehydes				citral, citronallal
Esters				geranyl acetate linalyl acetate methyl acetate
Ketones				itallidone thujone verbenone

Lactones			Used with caution	alpha-lactone
Oxide				1,8 cineole rose oxide
Phenols	Oregano, Thyme thymol, Savory		Skin irritant	carvacrol thymol
Phenylpropanes			Skin irritant Liver toxin at high dosages	cinnamic aldehyde euganol
Ether (Phenolpropane Derivatives) Properties Contraindications: Toxic to the nervous system at high dosages.				anethol methyl chavicol myristicin

1. List the healing properties for each essential oil.

Cedarwood: _____

Cape chamomile: _____

Eucalyptus: _____

Geranium: _____

Grapefruit: _____

Helichrysum: _____

Lavender: _____

Neroli: _____

Niaouli: _____

Palmarosa: _____

_____

Rosemary verbenone type: _____

Australian sandalwood: _____

Ylang ylang: _____

BLENDING ESSENTIAL OILS

List the uses of essential oils.

1. _____

2. _____

3. _____

4. _____

5. _____

6. _____

7. _____

CARRIER OILS

1. List the skin benefits for each carrier oil.

    a. Coconut oil: _____

    b. Jojoba oil: _____

    c. Kukui nut: _____

    d. Olive oil: _____

    e. Raspberry seed oil: _____

    f. Rose hip seed oil: _____

    g. Sunflower seed oil: _____

2. Search for the following terms in the word search puzzle below.

absolutes   isolate

allantoin   jojoba oil

emulsifier   phytotherapy

essential oil   refined

fixed oil   synergy

```
X  T  E  W  C  O  D  K  E  Q  V  C  G  D  S  O  E  O  I  X
Z  H  S  B  W  C  W  G  B  W  Z  X  H  Z  S  F  A  F  O  I
E  A  C  Y  P  M  E  B  E  T  R  E  R  W  Q  Y  I  Z  J  D
D  P  Y  G  E  E  B  U  K  K  S  F  M  Z  K  O  N  P  B  S
O  D  G  Z  D  H  M  I  A  C  C  P  U  Q  A  D  Z  P  W  E
K  R  R  G  E  L  A  Y  B  Q  E  U  U  Q  U  J  H  M  G  T
F  J  D  G  F  F  S  H  R  E  I  F  I  S  L  U  M  E  T  U
O  F  M  F  D  Z  O  K  C  E  N  B  V  J  G  Y  F  P  W  L
V  C  G  U  R  E  F  I  N  E  D  T  L  U  O  K  H  G  C  O
P  I  I  K  A  V  R  A  N  J  Y  Y  G  U  B  Y  T  G  M  S
C  E  S  S  E  N  T  I  A  L  O  I  L  F  T  W  P  W  B  B
H  B  P  T  X  U  G  R  N  V  R  I  Y  O  Q  K  I  H  S  A
Q  L  R  V  U  T  Y  I  X  W  W  E  T  Q  B  K  J  E  Y  E
H  T  M  L  T  H  X  J  C  C  T  H  G  I  S  B  Q  A  G  C
P  S  H  X  K  I  E  Z  C  M  E  Z  N  Z  R  U  U  X  R  I
N  I  O  T  N  A  L  L  A  R  F  I  X  E  D  O  I  L  E  K
P  T  H  T  C  Q  L  M  A  P  W  L  D  Z  S  P  G  V  N  M
F  G  A  N  D  U  S  P  Q  N  G  X  B  I  Q  K  R  K  Y  I
Z  I  C  N  C  B  Y  H  N  I  S  O  L  A  T  E  Z  Q  S  M
U  W  P  D  J  O  J  O  B  A  O  I  L  X  T  V  U  E  V  Z
```

14 INGREDIENTS AND PRODUCTS FOR SKIN ISSUES

Date: _____

Rating: _____

Text Pages: 305–322

CLEANSERS

Fill in the name of the type of cleanser that is associated with each description.

1. Clients with oily and combination skin are especially fond of a _____

2. Clients who have dry skin but still want the action of a foaming cleanser will use a

   _____

3. Clients who have very oily skin will like a _____

4. Clients who have mild to moderate acne will use a _____

   _____

5. Clients who have oily/combination skin may prefer a _____

   _____

6. Clients who have a typical combination skin will prefer a _____

7. Clients that have sensitive skin also prefer a _____

8. Clients that have dry, mature skin will benefit from the use of a _____

   _____

9. What is the active ingredient in a rinseable cleanser for oily and combination skin?

   _____

10. What is the active ingredient in a rinseable medicated cleanser for acne? _____

    _____

11. What is the active ingredient in a milk cleanser for oily and combination skin? _____

    _____

12. What is the active ingredient in cleansing milk for sensitive skin? _____

13. What is the active ingredient in cleansing milk for dry skin? _____

TONERS

Answer the following questions.

1. Name three reasons to use a toner.

    a. _____

    b. _____
        _____

    c. _____
        _____

2. Describe a toner for oily and combination skin.

    _____

3. Describe a toner for extremely oily skin.

    _____

4. Describe a toner for normal skin.

    _____
    _____
    _____

5. Describe a toner for extra-dry skin.

    _____
    _____

DAY CREAMS AND TREATMENTS

Answer the following questions.

1. What are the active ingredients in a day sunscreen protection fluid for oily and combination skin?

    _____
    _____
    _____
    _____
    _____

2. What are the active ingredients in a day cream for dry and dehydrated skin?

    _____
    _____
    _____

_____

_____

NIGHT CREAMS AND TREATMENTS

Answer the following questions.

1. What are the active ingredients in a night cream for oily-combination skin?

    _____

    _____

    _____

2. What are the active ingredients in a night cream for oily, clogged adult skin?

    _____

    _____

    _____

3. What are the active ingredients in a night hydrating cream for combination mature skin?

    _____

    _____

    _____

    _____

4. What are the active ingredients in a night cream for dry and dehydrated skin?

    _____

    _____

    _____

    _____

5. What are the active ingredients in a firming night cream for mature skin and lack of elasticity?

    _____

    _____

    _____

    _____

ABOUT AMPOULES AND SERUMS

Answer the following questions.

1. Active ingredients that are created for firming serum for mature skin with lack of elasticity
    are _____

2. Active ingredients that are created for lipid serum for wrinkles and dry skin are

_____

SPECIAL CREAMS AND TREATMENTS

Answer the following questions.

1. What are the product characteristics for an alpha hydroxy treatment for dry, sun-damaged skin?

_____

_____

_____

2. What are the product characteristics for an alpha hydroxy treatment gel for oily-combination, clogged skin?

_____

_____

_____

3. What are the product characteristics for a lightening gel for hyperpigmented skin?

_____

_____

_____

_____

4. What are the product characteristics for a benzoyl peroxide gel for acneic skin?

_____

_____

_____

5. List other specialized creams.

    a. _____

    b. _____

    c. _____

    d. _____

HOW PRODUCTS ARE DEVELOPED

1. Name the steps for developing a product.

    a. _____

    b. _____

c. _____

d. _____

e. _____

f. _____

g. _____

ADDITIONAL ROSACEA CARE TIPS

Answer the following questions.

1. What ingredients are good in sunscreens for rosacea?

    a. _____

    b. _____

2. Ingredients that reduce redness include:

    a. _____

    b. _____

    c. _____

    d. _____

    e. _____

    f. _____

    g. _____

    h. _____

    i. _____

    j. _____

    k. _____

    l. _____

    m. _____

    n. _____

15 PHARMACOLOGY FOR ESTHETICIANS

Date: _____

Rating: _____

Text Pages: 323–347

THE FDA AND DRUGS

Answer the following questions.

1. What does FDA stand for?

    _____

2. When and why did the FDA come into being?

    _____

    _____

3. What is the definition of a prescription?

    _____

    _____

PRESCRIPTION DRUGS

Fill in the information that is missing from the chart.

Category of Drug	Common Drug Names	Common Reasons for the Prescription
Antidepressants	Prozac, Zoloft	
Antivirals		
Antibiotics		
Antifungals		
Diuretics		
Hormones		
Hypoglycemic agents		Diabetes
Birth control medications	Many varieties	Prevent pregnancy
Anti-aging drugs		
Antibiotics	Cleocin-T	

Category of Drug	Common Drug Names	Common Reasons for the Prescription
Antivirals		
Anti-inflammatory drugs	Aclovate	

OVER-THE-COUNTER DRUGS

Fill in the information that is missing from the chart.

Category of Drug	Common Use	Common Products
Anti-aging medications	Accelerated epidermal turnover	
Pain medications		
Anti-diarrhea medications		Imodium AD

DRUG CATEGORIES

Fill in the information that is missing from the chart.

Drug Category	Expected Result	Drug Example
Analgesics (narcotic and non-narcotic)	Drugs to relieve pain	Narcotic: Morphine Non-narcotic: Aspirin
Antacids		
Antianxiety drugs		
Antiarrhythmics		
Antibiotics		
Anticoagulants		Coumadin
Anticonvulsants		Tegretol, Dilantin
Antidepressant		
Antidiarrheals		Lomotil
Antiemetics		
Antifungals	Treat fungal infection	
Antihistamines		
Antihypertensive		
Anti-inflammatory drugs	Reduce inflammation	
Antipsychotics		
Antipyretics	Reduce fever	Acetaminophen
Beta blockers		

Bronchodilators		
Corticosteroids		
Cough suppressants		HOLD Lozenges
Cytotoxics	Drugs to kill cells, used to treat cancer	Tamoxifien
Decongestants		
Diuretics		Lasix
Expectorant		
Hormones		estrogen, progesterone
Hypoglycemics		
Immunosuppressives		
Laxatives		Metamucil
Muscle relaxants		
Sleep drugs		Ambien
Thrombolytics		
Vitamins		

DRUGS USED TO TREAT HORMONAL IMBALANCES AND BIRTH CONTROL

List the hormones that bring on reactions shown in the first column.

Common Skin Effects	Various Hormones
rashes, acne, hirsutism, oily skin, itching, flushing, hyperpigmentation, hives	Calcitonin, Danazol,
acne, hirsutism, oily skin, rashes, itching, flushing, hyperpigmentation, hives	Estradiol acetate,

Common Skin Effects	Various Hormones

DRUGS USED TO TREAT BLOOD CONDITIONS

Fill in the information that is missing from the chart.

Drug Category	Example	Common Skin Effects
Lipid-lowering agents		
Thrombolytics	argatroban, bivalirudin, desirudin, lepirudin, antistreplase, streptokinase, tenecteplase	
Anticoagulants		
Antiplatelets	dalteparin, enoxaparin, fondaparinux, tinzaparin, eptifibatide, tirofiban	

DRUGS USED TO TREAT HEART CONDITIONS

1. Draw a line to match the terms to their definitions.

hypertension	By injection
acute coronary syndrome	Placed under the tongue
angina	High blood pressure
antianginals	Medical term for chest pain
sublingual	Problems associated with blood flow to the heart
parenteral	Drugs used to treat angina

2.   Fill in the information within the chart.

Drug Category	Example	Common Skin Effects
Beta blockers		
Calcium channel blockers	isradipine, nicardipine, verapamil	
Nitrates	isosorbide mononitrate, isosorbide dinitrate,	
Antiarrhythmics	disopyramide, moricizine, procainamide, quinidine, fosphenytoin, mexiletine, tocainide, acebutolol, diltiazem, atropine	
Antihypertensives	clonidine, eplerenone, benazepril, captopril, lisinopril, moexipril, ramipril, guanfacine, methyldopa,	

DRUGS USED TO TREAT LUNG DISORDERS

Draw a line to match the terms to their definitions.

antihistamines	A respiratory condition
antiasthmatics	Chemical mediator
bronchodilators	An example is levalbuterol
asthma	To prevent asthmatic conditions
antigen	Used to block histamine reactions
histamine	Invading substance

DRUGS USED TO TREAT GASTROINTESTINAL DISORDERS

Fill in the information that is missing from the chart.

Drug Category	Example	Common Skin Effects
Anticholinergics	atropine, darifenacin, dicyclomine, hyoscamine, oxybutynin, solifenacin, tolteradine	
Antidiarrheals	Bismuth subsalicylate, difenoxin/atropine,	
Antiemetics	dolasetron, ondansetron, granisetron	
Antiulcer		

DRUGS USED TO TREAT MENTAL DISORDERS

Answer the following questions.

1. List four panic disorders.

    a. _____

    b. _____

    c. _____

    d. _____

2. What type of medication would someone with epilepsy take? _____

3. List four different anticonvulsants.

    a. _____

    b. _____

c. _____

d. _____

4. Name three neurotransmitters.

a. _____

b. _____

c. _____

5. List the skin disorders that match the following group of medications:

Drug Category	Common Skin Effects
Antianxiety drugs	rashes
Anticonvulsants	
Antidepressants	
Antipsychotics	
Central nervous system stimulants	
Sedatives	

DRUGS USED TO TREAT DIABETES

Describe diabetes.

_____

_____

_____

DRUGS USED TO TREAT BACTERIAL, VIRAL, AND FUNGAL INFECTIONS

Answer the following questions.

1. What does MRSA stand for?

_____

2. What three pathogens can most skin infections be attributed to?

_____

3. What skin reactions can be caused by antibiotics?

_____

_____

4. Describe a virus.

_____

_____

5. List the skin conditions caused by antivirals.

_____

_____

6. What is a pathogenic fungus?

_____

_____

7. Give an example of superficial mycoses.

_____

8. List the skin conditions that oral antifungals can cause.

_____

_____

DRUGS USED TO TREAT SKELETAL CONDITIONS

Answer the following questions.

1. Which ethnic groups' members are more susceptible to osteoporosis?

_____

2. What skin effects do rheumatoid arthritis drugs cause?

_____

_____

3. How do corticosteroids function?

_____

_____

_____

4. What skin effects do corticosteroids have?

_____

_____

_____

_____

DRUGS USED TO TREAT PAIN

Fill in the missing information.

Drug Category	Common Skin Effects
Narcotic analgesics	
Non-steroidal anti-inflammatory agents (NSAIDS)	
Non-narcotic analgesics	
Muscle relaxants	

16 ADVANCED FACIAL TECHNIQUES

Date: _____

Rating: _____

Text Pages: 349–389

TREATMENT VARIATIONS

Describe the purpose for each step.

1. Cleanse: _____
   _____

2. Toners/Fresheners: _____
   _____
   _____

3. Water: _____
   _____

4. Exfoliation: _____
   _____
   _____
   _____

5. Massage: _____
   _____
   _____
   _____

6. Extraction: _____
   _____

7. Mask: _____
   _____

8. Penetration of ampoules or treatment serums: _____
   _____
   _____
   _____

9. Protection (moisturization and SPF): _____

_____

FOR DEHYDRATED SKIN

Fill in the missing steps for a facial for dehydrated skin.

1. Cleanse.

2. _____

3. Use hydrating ampoule.

4. _____

5. _____

6. Exfoliate.

7. Tone/freshen.

8. _____

9. _____

10. Use hydrating mask.

11. _____

12. Apply protection.

FOR CLOGGED RESISTIVE SKIN

Fill in the missing steps for a facial for clogged resistive skin.

1. Cleanse with massage to stimulate blood circulation.

2. Apply stripping toner (so that exfoliant will better penetrate).

3. _____

4. _____

5. Extract.

6. _____.

7. Use penetrating ampoules or serums.

8. _____

9. Apply protection.

FOR SENSITIVE SKIN

Fill in the missing steps for a facial for sensitive skin.

1. _____

2. Apply gentle toner/freshener.

3. Use soothing serum (to help skin tolerate exfoliation).

4. _____

5. _____

6. Use penetrating soothing serums or ampoules.

7. _____

8. Apply protection.

THERMOTHERAPY AND PRESSURE THEORY

Answer the following questions.

1. Explain three ways to apply thermotherapy.

    a. _____

    b. _____

    c. _____

2. Explain four ways to cool the skin.

    a. _____

    b. _____

    c. _____

    d. _____

3. How can you apply pressure therapy? _____

4.   What is the benefit of applying a refrigerator-cold towel? _____

_____

THERMOTHERAPY FOR CLOGGED PORES

Fill in the missing steps for a facial using thermotherapy for clogged pores.

1.   Prepare the client.

2.   Cleanse to remove makeup.

3.   Analysis and consultation.

4.   _____

5.   _____

6.   Extraction.

7.   Wipe the skin with an antiseptic toner.

8.   _____

9.   _____

10. Advise client to treat any extracted area carefully, avoiding touching it to minimize contamination with bacteria.

11. _____

12. _____

13. Follow clean-up and disinfection in accordance with state regulations.

14. _____

ROSACEA AND SENSITIVE SKIN TREATMENTS

List four concepts for sensitive skin.

1.   _____

2.   _____

3.   _____

_____

4.   _____

TREATMENT CONTRAINDICATIONS FOR TREATING SENSITIVE SKIN

For each statement about treating sensitive skin, write T for True or F for False.

1. __ Waxing should be avoided on sensitive skin.

2. __ Always use a high pH exfoliation chemical.

3. __ Perform a prolonged massage.

4. __ Avoid overdrying masks or leaving clay masks on too long.

5. __ Avoid heat exposure.

6. __ Microdermabrasion can be done for all clients that have sensitive skin.

7. __ Avoid paraffin.

8. __ Extractions can be for a prolonged amount of time.

9. __ Avoid using products containing isopropyl or SD alcohol.

10. __ Avoid heavily mentholated or alcohol-based treatment products.

11. __ Use non-fragranced products.

TREATMENT FOR SENSITIVE SKIN

Fill in the missing steps for a facial for sensitive skin.

1. Cleanse.

2. _____

3. Apply a lightweight, non-fragranced hydrating fluid.

4. _____

5. _____

6. Spray the skin with a mild, non-fragranced, non-alcohol toner.

7. Calm.

8. _____

9. Mask.

10. _____

CLIENT REACTIONS IN THE TREATMENT ROOM

Answer the following questions.

1. List some negative reactions that a client could have in the treatment room. _____

    _____

2. What should be done if a client has a negative reaction? _____

    _____

3. What are two examples of retinoids? _____

4. What is a normal side effect of using retinoids? _____

5. What should be avoided for someone who is on retinoids? _____

    _____

    _____

    _____

MANUAL MICRODERMABRASION

Fill in the missing steps for a facial using manual microdermabrasion.

1. Wash and disinfect hands.

2. _____

3. _____

4. Massage.

5. _____

6. Tone.

7. Treat.

8. _____

ENZYMES

Answer the following questions.

1. Enzymes are a proteolytic, which means they are _____

2. Enzyme peels are suitable for the following conditions:

a. _____

b. _____

c. _____

_____

d. _____

e. _____

_____

ACIDS

Answer the following questions.

1. List the characteristics of alpha hydroxy acids.

   a. _____

   b. _____

   c. _____

   d. _____

2. What is a beta hydroxy acid attracted to? _____

3. What is the highest strength of glycolic acid that an esthetician is allowed to use? _____

4. How does an acid peel help a client with strengthening his or her skin's elasticity? _____

   _____

   _____

   _____

5. Why is it important for a client to use products with alpha hydroxy acids prior to
   receiving a peel? _____

ALPHA HYDROXY ACID EXFOLIATIONS

Fill in the missing steps for a facial using exfoliating acids.

1. Cleanse the skin with makeup-removing cleanser.

2. _____

3. _____

4. Protection.

5. _____

6. _____

PRECAUTIONS FOR AHA EXFOLIATIONS

For each statement, write a T for True and an F for False.

1. ___ Always make sure the skin has been pretreated with lower-strength alpha hydroxy acid at home for at least 2 weeks before administering 30% AHA treatment.

2. ___ After waxing, wait at least 24 hours before performing an AHA treatment.

3. ___ It is permissible to perform an AHA treatment on anyone with a skin disorder.

4. ___ Do not use the peeling agent on a male client immediately after he has shaved.

5. ___ Accutane patients can receive AHA treatments.

6. ___ Do not use AHAs on someone who is using keratolytics.

7. ___ If the skin is irritated, it is permissible to use AHAs.

8. ___ If the client has a history of herpes simplex, refer him or her to a doctor.

9. ___ Clients do not have to wear sunscreen after receiving an AHA treatment.

10. ___ Check with a client to see how his or her skin has reacted in past treatments (if any).

TREATMENTS FOR HYPERPIGMENTED SKIN AND SUPERFICIAL PEELS

Answer the following questions.

1. Treatments for hyperpigmented skin can include: _____
   _____

2. Most experienced professionals agree that TCA belongs in the hands of dermatologists and _____

3. A superficial peel can remove cells from the _____ only.

4. An example of a superficial peel is called a _____

5. What type of client would benefit from a clinic deep exfoliation? _____

_____

6. What type of clients should not have chemical peeling performed?

   a. _____

   b. _____

   c. _____

   _____

   _____

7. The following clients should have written permission from a physician to receive a chemical peeling treatment.

   a. _____

   b. _____

   c. _____

   d. _____

8. What are the benefits of a superficial peel? _____

   _____

   _____

PROCEDURE FOR CHEMICAL PEELS

Fill in the missing steps for a facial using chemical peels.

1. Complete the pre-exfoliation consultation procedure.

2. _____

3. _____

4. Put on gloves.

5. Perform a second cleansing.

6. _____

7. Apply occlusive barriers.

8. _____

9. Apply the liquid solution on the face.

10. Place a small fan so that it blows gently on the client's face.

11. _____

12. Rinse frost and residue from the skin using a neutralizer as recommended.

13. _____

MASK THERAPIES

Fill in the chart below.

Suffocation	Triggering increased circulation to the area
	Adding moisture
	Purging, drawing, absorption of impurities
	Soothing
	Rejuvenating
	Smoothing the skin

APPLICATION OF A POWDER MASK

Fill in the missing steps for applying a powder mask.

1. Apply appropriate serums for the skin.

2. Apply a layer of moisturizer to skin.

3. _____

4. _____

5. Apply damp cotton rounds to protect the eye area.

6. Apply a single-layer gauze sheet over the client's face to facilitate removal.

7. _____

8. _____

9. Remove the mask by placing your fingers along the hairline perimeter of mask just above jaw level.

10. _____

11. Apply sun protection.

ADVANCED SKIN CARE MASSAGE

Date: _____

Rating: _____

Text Pages: 390–434

ADVANCED FACIAL MOVEMENTS

Answer the following questions.

1. List a few of the specialty massages.

   a. _____

   b. _____

   c. _____

2. List the seven contraindications for massage.

   a. _____

   b. _____

   c. _____

   d. _____

   e. _____

   f. _____

   g. _____

3. What are the key components to a massage?

   a. _____

   b. _____

   c. _____

SELECTING AND INCORPORATING ADVANCED FACIAL MOVEMENTS

Describe how to perform each of these massage techniques in your own words:

1. Eye Express: _____

    _____

2. Around We Go: _____

    _____

    _____

    _____

    _____

3. Center Point: _____

    _____

    _____

    _____

4. Sinus Relief: _____

    _____

    _____

    _____

    _____

    _____

5. Paddle Wheel: _____

    _____

    _____

    _____

6. Feather Off: _____

    _____

7. Forehead Press: _____

    _____

8. Gallop 1-2-1: _____

    _____

    _____

    _____

9. Full Face Sweep: _____

    _____

10. Rolling Along: _____

    _____

_____

_____

11. Feels Good: _____

_____

_____

_____

_____

12. Décolleté Sweep: _____

_____

_____

_____

13. Ski Up: _____

14. Neck-Shoulder-Arm: _____

_____

_____

_____

_____

15. Rock-a-bye: _____

_____

_____

ADVANCED BACK MOVEMENTS

List the two advanced back movements:

1. _____

2. _____

SHIATSU MASSAGE FOR THE FACE

When performing Shiatsu, it is important to remember the following.

1. _____

2. _____

_____

3. _____

4. _____

Each touch in Shiatsu is performed to the count of three:

1. _____

2. _____

3. _____

PROCEDURE FOR THE SHIATSU MASSAGE FOR HEAD AND NECK

Fill in the missing steps.

Preparation

1. Set up the facial lounge and prepare the room for the client.

2. Decant massage vehicle, if desired.

3. Before the client gets onto the lounge, allow him or her to put on a gown.

4. _____

Procedure

5. _____

6. Glide your hands up over the face to the forehead.

7. Begin at the top of the head, running your fingers through the hair.

8. Running Water

9. Down River

10. _____

11. _____

12. Bright Eyes

13. _____

14. _____

15. Rinse Away

REFLEXOLOGY FOR THE FACE AND EARS

Answer the following questions.

1. Explain reflexology for the face.

_____

_____

_____

_____

_____

2. Explain ear reflexology.

_____

_____

_____

_____

STONES MASSAGE FOR ESTHETICIAN

Answer the following questions.

1. Explain warm stone massage:

_____

_____

_____

_____

_____

_____

2. How would cold stones be beneficial?

_____

_____

STONES MASSAGE PROCEDURE

Fill in the missing steps in the procedure for stone massage for face.

Preparation

1. Set up the facial lounge in the typical manner and prepare the treatment room for client.

2. Gather supplies for the facial treatment.

3. _____

4. Turn on the stone warming unit and heat following manufacturer's guidelines.

5. Perform all massage steps of the facial before starting the stone massage. Apply massage vehicle.

6. _____

7. Turn on the steamer if you choose to use it during the massage.

Procedure

1. _____

2. _____
   _____

3. When stones feel comfortable to handle, test one against the client's skin to assure that the temperature is comfortable for the client.

4. Start at the corrigator with one stone held between the thumb and first finger of each hand.

5. _____

6. _____

7. Glide stones along the perimeter of the face to meet at the center of the chin.

8. _____

9. Simultaneously perform circles, moving from the chin along the jawline to the ears.

10. Using both hands simultaneously, glide up and repeat this process in the hollow above the jawline along the lower teeth moving from the chin to the ears.

11. _____

12. Alternating hands, perform strokes from the corners of the nose, across the cheeks, and back toward the temples, starting on the right side of the nose. Repeat on the left side of the face.

13. Repeat steps 10 through 12 three times, and then glide your hands to the temples.

14. _____
    _____

15. _____

16. Moving both hands simultaneously, glide from the top of the nose up over the brow.

17. Alternating hands, stroke up the neck to jawline, starting on the right side of the face.

18. _____
_____
_____

19. From the temple on the right side, continue feathering strokes to the hairline. _____

20. _____
_____

21. Glide stones so each hand is positioned at the base of each ear. _____

22. _____
_____

23. Finish by stroking stones simultaneously off each shoulder. _____

LYMPHATIC MASSAGE FOR THE FACE AND NECK

Fill in the blanks using the word bank below.

bruising	injury
healing crisis	lymph
infections	lymphocytes
lymph nodes	skillful directed touch

1. The head and neck are rich with _____ , because disease-causing organisms easily enter the body via the mouth, nose, and eyes.

2. Lymph drainage massage stimulates the circulation of lymph and _____ through the facial and cervical lymph nodes.

3. LDM to the face and neck effectively reduces _____ and edema following injury or surgery, including dental and cosmetic surgery.

4. Facial edema can be due to allergies, hormones, medication, fatigue, illness, infection, _____ , excess salt in the diet, weeping and so on.

5. LDM stimulates a sluggish immune system to more activity by increasing the circulation of _____ and _____

6. Although LDM is focused on superficial tissues, the muscles underneath also respond to the light, _____ and will relax.

7. Many people have chronically swollen lymph nodes, often from repeated _____ and childhood illness.

8. A _____ means simply that the client might experience a flare-up of old symptoms.

9. Unscramble the following names of the lymph nodes.

ucularria   _____

stnmubeal   _____

msibdarunbula   _____

ntraerio viccealr naihc   _____

rioportse relvciac hinac   _____

PROCEDURE FOR LYMPHATIC DRAINAGE MASSAGE

Fill in the missing steps in the procedure for LDM for the neck.

Preparation

1. Consult with the client to assure there are no contraindications to treatment and to complete all intake forms.

2. Assure the client has signed informed consent to service.

3. _____

4. Offer a bolster if the client needs one under his or her knees.

Procedure

1. Sit or stand at the client's head.

2. Apply skin-cleansing agent.

3. _____

4. As the towel cools, massage gently through the towel to relax the tissues. Before removing the towel, use it to gently wipe the face and to prevent massaging any cosmetics or dirt particles into the skin.

5. _____

6. _____

7. Perform 20 stationary circles on the subauricular nodes, between the ears and the mastoid process, posterior and inferior to the ears. Use three or four fingers, flat against the skin, to stretch the skin gently in a circular direction, counting each circle carefully to keep the pace very slow. This takes nearly 3 minutes.

8. _____
   _____
   _____
   _____

9. Repeat Step 6 on the posterior chain of cervical nodes.

10. Slide the flat pads of fingers of both hands under the neck, covering the skin from the bottom of the neck and hairline. Perform 7 stationary circles, moving the skin on the back of the neck over the cervical vertebrae.

11. _____
    _____

12. Place two flat fingers inside the triangle by the sternocleidomastoid muscle, the clavicle, and the scalene muscles, and again perform stationary circles for a full minute.

13. _____

14. _____
    _____

Caution: Omit Steps 15, 16, and 17 (the front of the neck) for any client who has thyroid abnormalities.

15. Place flat fingertips in the depression between the thyroid cartilage and the sternocleidomastoid muscles, and perform rotary massage using very light pressure.

16. _____
    _____

17. Effleurage the throat and the back of the neck. The direction of pressure follows lymph drainage.

18 ADVANCED FACIAL DEVICES

Date: _____

Rating: _____

Text Pages: 435–474

INTRODUCTION

Look for the following terms in the word search puzzle below.

LED Devices   IPL   Photodynamic   Ultrasonic
Skin Analysis devices   Electro Dessication   Microcurrent

```
A  D  A  J  V  D  A  U  J  I  U  Z  K  P  T  L  G  S  T  N
O  O  C  N  F  P  H  L  P  E  Y  G  Y  U  N  L  Y  Z  S  H
R  S  V  C  A  Z  W  T  O  L  B  M  O  W  D  D  Z  K  I  B
X  N  K  V  S  M  J  R  P  E  Y  G  O  D  B  X  I  F  G  K
X  K  W  W  E  H  C  A  M  C  O  Z  F  T  K  N  R  L  T  M
E  K  Q  Z  R  E  L  S  Y  T  E  L  N  K  A  M  S  N  L  U
S  X  Y  L  H  V  H  O  E  R  Y  M  T  N  Y  N  E  P  F  A
P  C  B  B  D  O  R  N  B  O  I  Y  A  B  W  R  I  C  L  W
I  U  J  I  A  G  A  I  R  D  O  L  C  H  R  M  I  C  W  L
C  Z  H  L  U  K  A  C  Y  E  Y  J  L  U  O  M  D  H  U  H
L  E  D  D  E  V  I  C  E  S  C  B  C  U  A  U  P  Y  N  L
X  F  F  N  P  I  J  W  I  S  X  O  E  N  L  W  K  A  K  H
S  P  L  L  Z  R  K  S  T  I  R  A  Y  V  S  U  N  F  Z  C
Q  Y  Z  L  G  W  D  V  X  C  D  D  Q  L  S  W  L  X  X  B
N  K  C  I  V  E  V  V  I  A  O  W  M  E  K  V  K  A  V  H
I  I  A  P  V  Y  C  M  V  T  D  C  U  U  J  M  L  L  J  W
B  Z  Q  I  P  U  X  L  O  I  W  V  A  X  B  Q  G  V  I  R
H  U  C  D  W  H  K  Y  H  M  O  R  R  I  D  B  Q  V  C  C  E
O  E  K  H  K  G  P  C  A  N  I  T  U  R  O  A  L  O  O  D
S  W  E  Q  Q  W  M  B  G  U  B  J  Q  W  F  L  S  Q  S  K
```

THE PURCHASING PROCESS

Answer the following questions.

1. An esthetician performing such services needs to contact his or her _____

2. List what you would consider when analyzing your practice needs.

    a. _____

    b. _____

    c. _____

    d. _____

    e. _____

    f. _____

3. In your own words, state how you would research the best manufacturer.

    _____

    _____

4. What should you consider when it comes to maintenance and disposable/reusable parts?

    _____

    _____

    _____

5. What forms of training might a manufacturer offer?

    _____

6. What types of labels would be on various machines?

    _____

SKIN ANALYSIS DEVICES

Answer the following questions.

1. Explain the research by Patrick Bitters, M.D.

    _____

    _____

    _____

2. Explain the research by Robert Weiss, M.D.

    _____

    _____

_____
_____
_____
_____

FACIAL REJUVENATION

Answer the following questions.

1. Describe photorejuvenation. _____
    _____

2. IPL facial rejuvenation has become the gold standard due to the _____ noncoherent, _____ flashlamp effects.

3. During the procedure, intense white light is pulsed with wavelengths ranging from _____ in the energy spectrum.

4. List the common conditions that can be treated with IPL device for photorejuvenation.

    a. _____

    b. _____

    c. _____

    d. _____

    e. _____

    f. _____

    g. _____

THE CONSULTATION

Answer the following questions.

1. What are some medical issues that you need to ask a client about during the consultation?

    a. _____

    b. _____

    c. _____

    d. _____

e. _____

f. _____

g. _____

h. _____

i. _____

j. _____

k. _____

2. What tool should you use to evaluate a client's skin type?

_____

3. List examples of "red flag" clients.

a. _____
_____

b. _____

c. _____
_____

d. _____
_____

e. _____
_____

4. Name some antibiotics that can be photosensitizing.

a. _____

b. _____

c. _____

5. List the possible contraindications to treatment.

a. _____

b. _____

c. _____

d. _____

e. _____
_____

f. _____

g. _____

h. _____

i. _____

j. _____

k. _____

IPL PHOTOREJUVENATION

Unscramble the names of the following implements and materials used in an IPL photorejuvenation procedure.

resncale _____

eiltcn rpead _____

lge olconat _____

uns roetpiotnc _____

rewta wolb _____

rneot _____

tops-retatnetm mures _____

evlogs _____

eldssibaop pogsens _____

rottviepce weyaere _____

avaltinoeu msrof _____

Fill in the missing steps in the following procedure.

Preparation

1. Prepare treatment lounge and client gown.

2. Assemble towels and disposables.

3. Set up products and protective devices.

4. Have the appropriate sign for the outside door ready.

5. Hand client post-care instructions. These can be discussed while any anesthetics absorb.

6. _____
   _____

7. _____

8. Hang up the appropriate eyewear on the door for staff who may enter.

9. Turn on the IPL machine. _____

10. _____

11. Replace any IPL handpieces and filters that need replacing.

Procedure

1. Secure client's hair away from the face.

2. _____

3. _____

4. _____

5. Ask if the client has tanned recently or used self-tanner within the last month.

6. Reconfirm areas of treatment and the client's goals.

7. _____

8. Take documentary photographs.

9. Enter the client's demographic data into the IPL system, if required by device.

10. _____
    _____

11. Double-check all parameters before treating.

12. _____

13. Put on gloves.

14. _____

15. _____

16. Float the filter in the gel if this is appropriate for your specific device.

17. After testing the spot, assess clinical end points.

18. If the test response is acceptable, continue treatment with the same settings.

19. Start treatment with the forehead.

20. _____

21. Place the handpiece perpendicular to the skin and floating in the gel, if one is required by the manufacturer.

22. Fire trigger.

23. _____

24. _____

25. _____

26. _____

27. Move to the nose, upper lip. and chin in a systematic manner. Then move to below and above the lips, being careful not to work over lip vermillion.

28. Progress to the cheeks and treat across the cheeks in a systematic manner.

29. Remove any residual gel.

30. _____

31. Apply soothing agent and protective sunscreen.

Post-procedure

1. Supply the client with an ice pack, if recommended or needed.

2. Client is escorted to the front office for fees processing and scheduling of additional treatments and/or follow-ups.

3. _____

4. _____

Clean-up and Disinfection

1. Turn off machine with the key following manufacturer guidelines.

2. Wipe down the machine with germicidal wipes.

3. _____

4. _____
   _____

5. Follow clean-up and sanitation procedures in accordance with state guidelines.

6. Reset and prepare the room for the next client.

7. _____

LIGHT-EMITTING DIODES (LEDS)

Answer the following questions.

1. Explain a service using a LED Device:

   _____
   _____
   _____
   _____

2. What can be treated with the LED Device?

   a. _____

   b. _____

   c. _____

   d. _____

   e. _____

3. What are the contraindications to an LED Treatment?

   a. _____

   b. _____

   c. _____

d. _____

e. _____

f. _____

PHOTODYNAMIC THERAPY

Answer the following questions.

1. Photodynamic therapy is used with a photosensitizing drug enhancer called

_____

2. What is this treatment used for?

_____

3. How is this procedure performed?

_____

_____

_____

MICRODERMABRASION

Answer the following questions.

1. When was microdermabrasion introduced? _____

2. What has microdermabrasion been documented to help with?

a. _____

b. _____

c. _____

3. What are the two grades of microdermabrasion machines?

_____

4. Explain the various types of machines.

a. Aluminum Oxide Crystals: _____

_____

_____

_____

_____

b. Organic Crystals: _____

_____

_____

_____

_____

_____

_____

_____

_____

_____

c. Non-Crystal Devices: _____

_____

_____

_____

_____

_____

_____

d. Vibrating Ultrasonic Paddles: _____

_____

_____

_____

_____

5. List some of the skin problems that microdermabrasion may help.

a. _____

b. _____

_____

c. _____

d. _____

e. _____

6. List possible contraindications:

a. _____

b. _____

c. _____

d. _____

e. _____

f. _____

g. _____

h. _____

i. _____

MICRODERMABRASION PROCEDURE

Fill in the missing steps for a microdermabrasion procedure.

1. Position the client comfortably in relaxing, reclining position with hair protected.

2. Make sure the client has removed all facial piercings, jewelry, and contact lenses.

3. _____

4. _____

5. Dry the skin.

6. Protect client's eyes with occlusive adhesive eyewear, pads, or moistened gauze.

7. _____

8. Follow manufacturer's recommendations for pressure settings, time exposure, and treatment protocol.

9. _____

10. _____
    _____

11. _____
    _____

12. Repeat both sets of passes on the other side of forehead.

13. Repeat both sets of passes on each cheek, working from the nose to jaw outward, and from the orbital bone to the chin.

14. Repeat both sets of passes on the chin.

15. _____

16. _____

_____ Use the orbital bone as a guideline for how close to the eyes to go. _____

_____

_____

_____

17. After completing all microdermabrasion, brush away any loose crystals.

18. Rinse the face to ensure that you have removed all crystals.

19. _____

20. Conclude the treatment with soothing serum or lotion and sun protection.

ULTRASONIC TECHNOLOGY

Answer the following questions.

1. What does ultrasonic technology use to clean out pores? _____

2. How is product penetration achieved? _____

_____

_____

3. What is another name for the peel modality? _____

ULTRASONIC FACIAL

Fill in the missing steps of the following procedure.

Part I

1. Drape the client and secure hair away from the face.

2. Pre-cleanse and remove makeup using a water-based cleanser.

3. Adjust machine settings per manufacturer instructions and based on client skin type.

4. Apply cleanser, combined with a small trace of water for moisture, and apply to the client's face in small, circular motions, leaving the area slightly wet.

5. Attach the wristband to the client and insert ear pads and eye pads for protection, if required by your state regulations.

6. _____

7. _____

8. Starting with the forehead, gently secure/stretch the skin to be treated, between your thumb and pointer finger, just as when you perform a microdermabrasion treatment.

9. _____
_____

10. Move to the right cheek and repeat movements.

11. _____

12. Ask the client to hold his or her lips in a compressed "M" while you stroke across and downward from the nose toward the upper lip.

13. Stroke downward on the nose.

14. Use the corner of blade to stroke around the nasal flares.

15. _____

Part II

1. _____

2. _____

3. As in Part I, start with the forehead. If the skin shows signs of laxity, isolate areas in the same manner.

4. _____

5. _____
_____
_____

6. Increase or decrease intensity as indicated by the manufacturer.

7. _____

8. _____

9. Move to the cheeks, chin, and the center of the face, repeating the process.

10. When you have treated the entire face, either move to the micro-amp phase of unit operations or conclude with a moisturizer and sun protection.

Part III

1. Some ultrasonic units have settings specifically for the micro-amp or homeostasis phase.

2. _____

3. _____

4. _____
    _____

5. Rinse off excess gel with warm, moist towel.

6. _____

7. Inform the client about appropriate home care.

8. _____

9. Perform clean-up and disinfection according to state regulations.

10. _____
    _____

ELECTRODESSICATION DEVICES (RADIO FREQUENCY)

Answer the following questions.

1. What are electrodessication devices used for?

    a. _____

    b. _____

    c. _____

    d. _____

    e. _____

    f. _____

2. List contraindications for electrodessication.

    a. _____

    b. _____

c. _____

d. _____

e. _____

f. _____

g. _____

h. _____

i. _____

j. _____

ELECTRODESSICATION PROCEDURE

Fill in the missing steps for this electrodessication procedure.

Procedure

1. Wash your hands and put on gloves.

2. _____

3. Wipe the client's skin with antiseptic solution on a 2×2 gauze pad and allow it to dry completely.

4. Manufacturer's directions may require the client to hold a ground as with galvanic facial therapies. Treatment parameters vary by device; follow the manufacturer's recommendations.

5. _____

6. _____

7. As low-level radio-frequency/direct current pass through the probe to the vessel or target lesion, look for blanching or coagulation of the vessel or targeted lesion.

8. _____
   _____

Post-procedure

1. The client's skin may be tender after treatment. Tell the client not to disturb lesions or vessels for 24 hours.

2. If the manufacturer or supervising physician recommends it, apply an antibacterial ointment to the treated area.

3. Use only soothing and hydrating products.

4. _____
    _____

5. _____
    _____
    _____

6. For treatments in the facial area, advise the client to abstain from washing, rubbing or patting the face for the first 12 hours.

7. Document the equipment settings used for the client's treatment in treatment record sheets.

MICROCURRENT "FACIAL TONING"

Answer the following questions.

1. What benefit can microcurrent offer? _____

2. What type of currents does microcurrent use? _____

3. What is the conductor for transferring the current? _____

INDICATIONS FOR TREATMENT

Fill in the blanks in the following chart.

Desired Treatment	Muscle Group	Technique
Reduction of eyelid hooding and brow drooping	Orbicularis oculi muscle closes the eyelid and compresses the lacrimal sac (tear duct)	Lifting, strengthening, and tightening
Reduction of jawline laxity and skin drooping		
Reduction of furrowing and lines between brows		Relaxing and lengthening
Reduction of furrowing and lines between brows		

Desired Treatment	Muscle Group	Technique
Reduction of forehead lines and laxity		
Reduction of marionette lines	Risorius muscle retracts the mouth.	Lifting, strengthening, and tightening
Reduction of marionette lines		

CONTRAINDICATIONS TO TREATMENT

What are the contraindications to microcurrent?

1. _____

2. _____

3. _____

4. _____

5. _____

6. _____

7. _____

8. _____

9. _____

MANAGEMENT OF COMPLICATIONS

Fill in the following chart.

Side Effect	Possible Interventions
Excessive swelling	
Excessive skin reaction	

Side Effect	Possible Interventions
Blistering or crusting	
Hyperpigmentation	
Hypopigmentation	
Infection	Physician may order antibiotic, antiviral, or antifungal medications.
Scarring	

19 HAIR REMOVAL

Date: _____

Rating: _____

Text Pages: 475–517

SAFETY AND DISINFECTION FIRST

Answer the following questions.

1. During a hair removal procedure, when should you wear gloves?

    _____

2. If a client has a history of the herpes virus, what should the client do?

    _____

3. Genital warts are a viral infection caused by the human papilloma virus. If you see this
    condition on a client who comes in for a bikini wax, what should you do?

    _____

4. Why is pregnancy a contraindication for a hair removal treament?

    _____

    _____

THREADING

1. Fill in the blanks in the following questions with the words from the word bank.

    banding   khite
    faster rate   looped and twisted
    fatlah   skin

    a. Threading is also known as _____

    b. Threading is a method of hair removal that uses a _____ cotton thread
        maneuvered by the technician's fingers

    c. Threading does not cause trauma to the _____

    d. In Arabic, threading is known as _____ and, in Egyptian, _____

    e. Threading is mass tweezing, but is accomplished at a much _____ then tweezing.

2. Explain the preparation of equipment and treatment area.

_____

_____

_____

3. Explain how you should prepare a client for a treatment.

_____

_____

_____

_____

_____

4. How long should the thread be? _____

SUGARING

Answer the following questions.

1. Where has sugaring been used for centuries? _____

_____

2. How long does the hair need to be? _____

3. What is the downside to sugaring? _____

4. What is the downside to the spatula applied method? _____

_____

5. What are the benefits of sugaring?

a. _____

b. _____

_____

_____

_____

c. _____

_____

_____

_____

d. _____

_____

e. _____
_____
_____

f. _____
_____

g. _____

h. _____
_____

i. _____

j. _____

k. _____

6.   Explain how the sugar paste would be applied to the skin.

_____
_____
_____
_____
_____

HARD WAX

Answer the following questions.

1.   Why did hard wax make a comeback?

_____
_____

2.   What should the temperature be on the hard wax warmer?

_____

3.   Depilatory waxes are often made up of beeswax, candelilla wax, and _____

4.   How should strip wax be applied?

_____
_____
_____
_____

SOFT WAX

Answer the following questions.

1. Why is soft wax the most popular method?

    _____

    _____

2. What are some soothing ingredients found in soft wax?

    _____

3. Why would a client experience small pustules a few days after a lip wax?

    _____

    _____

    _____

4. What type of treatment would help ingrown hairs?

    _____

ADVANCE FACIAL WAXING

Answer the following questions.

1. On the illustration below, mark the direction you would measure for the beginning, arch, and end of the eyebrow.

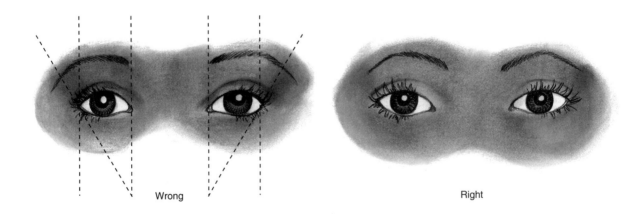

Wrong   Right

2. Draw the correct eyebrows on each face shape.

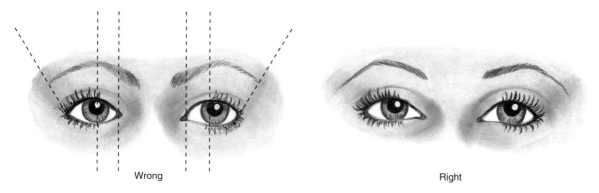

Wrong   Right

3. What type of wax is better for waxing the sides of the face and why?

_____

_____

SPEED WAXING AND BODY TECHNIQUES

Answer the following questions.

1. How is speed waxing accomplished?

_____

_____

2. In order to be an effective speed waxer, what should you do first?

_____

3. What is the most effective way to remove hair from the arms? _____

4. What is the most preferred method to wax the hands? _____

5. Describe the American bikini wax.

_____

_____

6. Describe a French bikini wax.

_____

_____

_____

7. Describe a Brazilian bikini wax.

_____

THE BRAZILIAN WAX PROCEDURE

Fill in the missing steps for the Brazilian wax procedure.

Procedure

1. Wash hands and put on the gloves and apron.

2. Help the client onto the bed and ask her to assume a supine (faceup) position.

3. _____
    _____

4. Cleanse the upper leg and the bikini area with an antiseptic cleanser and pat dry.

5. _____

6. Offer the client gloves.

7. _____
    _____

8. Starting to work first on the right side of the client's bikini area, have the client place the *left* hand firmly on the skin, stretching with fingers straight downward. Client should wear gloves when assisting with the stretching.

9. _____

10. Working on the bent leg, apply the wax with the edge of a spatula in the direction of hair growth. The first application should be to the section farthest away from the bikini line and only up to the femoral ridge, following the downward direction of hair growth.

11. _____
    _____
    _____

12. Apply immediate, firm pressure to alleviate the discomfort.

13. Repeat this process working toward the bikini line.

14. Repeat on left side of client's bikini.

15. _____

16. _____
    _____
    _____
    _____

17. Move to the pubis. Apply wax in direction of growth in 1-by-3-inch segments.

18. Allow wax to set and remove it, followed by pressure.

19. _____

20. _____
    _____

21. _____
    _____

22. Have the client lift one leg toward her chest, grasping the ankle with the opposite hand and drawing the leg across the body. This should expose the last remaining third of the hair that was too near the table to apply the wax. This position also ensures that the skin is nice and taut. The wax is applied as before, downward, with the pull upward.

23. _____
    _____

24. Use soothing antiseptic lotion on the entire area that has been waxed.

25. _____

26. Have the client turn over into a kneeling prone position with one forearm resting on the table in front of her. This allows the client a free hand to move the panties to one side and to help separate the buttocks.

27. Use preparatory disinfectant on the area and apply powder.

28. _____
    _____
    _____

29. Allow the wax to set, and then remove against growth.

30. _____

31. _____
    _____

32. _____
    _____

33. When you have removed all hair, use soothing antiseptic lotion and ensure that you have removed any residual wax.

ADVANCED MALE WAXING

1. List the areas where men usually get waxed.

   a. _____

   b. _____

   c. _____

   d. _____

2. List the two areas that male swimmers get waxed.

   a. _____

   b. _____

3. Describe an eyebrow wax for a man.

   _____

   _____

   _____

   _____

   _____

   _____

4. In which direction should you wax a back?

   _____

5. Explain how to wax a man's ears.

   _____

   _____

   _____

   _____

LASER AND PULSED LIGHT HAIR REMOVAL

Fill in the chart below

Laser or Light	Skin Type	Hair Color	Type of Hair
Pulsed Diode	I–IV		Prefers coarse
Ruby			Fine and coarse

Laser or Light	Skin Type	Hair Color	Type of Hair
Normal mode Nd:YAG			
Q-switched Nd:YAG	I–VI (temporary removal only)		
Alexandrite			Fine and coarse
Intense Pulse Light		Black to light brown	

INTENSE PULSED LIGHT

Fill in the blanks using terms from the word bank below.

1,000 nm   pigment
hair reduction   polychromatic
nonablative

1. Intense pulsed light is _____ and broadband.

2. The wavelength on an intense pulsed light is between 400 nm to _____

3. The filters that are used create wavelengths that selectively target different skin structures—hair, _____, or vessels.

4. Some IPL devices have demonstrated efficiency in _____

5. IPL treatments are gaining in popularity because they are _____, more comfortable, faster and less expensive for both the client and the practitioner.

6. List the benefits of laser or IPL hair removal vs. other treatment modalities.

   a. _____
   b. _____
   c. _____
   _____
   d. _____
   _____
   e. _____
   f. _____

7. List the downsides of laser or IPL hair removal vs. other treatment modalities.

   a. _____

   b. _____

   c. _____

   d. _____

   e. _____

   f. _____

   g. _____

   h. _____
   _____

8. List four safety guidelines for the laser room.

   a. _____

   b. _____

   c. _____

   d. _____

9. List five safety guidelines for the technician in the laser room.

   a. _____

   b. _____

   c. _____

   d. _____

   e. _____

10. What are the four main categories of excess hair growth?

   a. _____

   b. _____

   c. _____

   d. _____

11. What is hypertrichosis?

_____

12. What is hirsutism?

_____

13. What is a hair-bearing flap?

_____

_____

14. What is a cosmetic reason for wanting hair removal?

_____

15. What is the most important conversation you can have with your client?

_____

_____

16. What are the contraindications for laser hair removal?

_____

_____

_____

Fill in the chart below.

Fitzpatrick Skin Type	Description	Laser Hair Removal Considerations
Type I	Very fair skin accompanied by blonde or light-red hair and blue or green eyes; never tans, always burns.	
Type II	Fair skin accompanied by light-brown or red hair and green, blue or brown eyes. Occasionally tans, always burns.	
Type III	Medium skin accompanied by brown hair and brown eyes;	
Type IV	Olive skin, accompanied by brown hair and brown eyes; often tans, sometimes burns	

Fitzpatrick Skin Type	Description	Laser Hair Removal Considerations
Type V	Dark-brown skin accompanied by black hair and black eyes;	
Type VI	Black skin accompanied by black hair and black eyes;	

THE CONSULATION

1. List the important information to discuss with a client before a laser hair removal treatment.

    a. _____

    b. _____

    c. _____

    d. _____

    e. _____

    f. _____

    g. _____

    h. _____

2. List the steps to complete prior to treatment:

    a. _____
        _____

    b. _____

    c. _____

    d. _____

e. _____

f. _____

THE LASER HAIR REMOVAL TREATMENT PROCEDURE

Fill in the missing steps in the laser hair removal procedure.

1. Unlock the laser device.

2. _____

3. _____

4. Set the treatment parameters according to manufacturer's guidelines or charted settings from previous treatment for the area, hair, and skin according to the response at the test site.

5. _____
   _____
   _____
   _____

6. Compress the skin firmly with the handpiece to disperse the oxyhemoglobin (a chromophore that competes with melanin) away from the treatment area. Doing so allows for greater absorption of the laser light and reduces the risk of epidermal damage, as well as maneuvers the dermal papilla closer to the surface, which makes for a more effective treatment.

7. _____

8. _____
   _____

9. _____
   _____
   _____
   _____
   _____

10. Read the skin. If topical anesthesia and cooling remedies have not reduced the client's discomfort, make adjustments.

11. _____

12. After treating the entire area, wipe down the skin with soothing antiseptic lotion.

THE LASER HAIR REMOVAL TREATMENT

Answer the following questions.

1. What is a drawback of using a topical anesthesia? _____

_____

_____

_____

2. What are the technical issues that affect the overall result of the hair removal process?

_____

_____

3. How can the skin be cooled during the treatments? _____

4. What is the spot size? _____

5. Describe wavelength? _____

_____

_____

6. How is the energy fluence measured? _____

7. What does thermal storage coefficient mean? _____

8. What is the pulse duration (or pulse width)? _____

_____

9. Describe thermal relaxation time. _____

_____

10. List the home care directions.

   a. _____

   _____

   b. _____

   _____

   c. _____

   _____

   d. _____

   _____

   _____

e. _____
_____
_____

f. _____
_____
_____
_____

g. _____
_____
_____

h. _____
_____

i. _____
_____

11. List the treatment consequences of laser hair removal:

a. _____
_____

b. _____
_____

c. _____

12. Complications of laser hair removal include:

a. _____

b. _____

c. _____

d. _____

e. _____

13. How do you minimize liability concerns? _____
_____

20 ADVANCED MAKEUP

Date: _____

Rating: _____

Text Pages: 518–561

SEMIPERMANENT EYELASH EXTENSIONS

Answer the following questions using the word bank below.

1/3	disposables
two	flush
catagen	pregnancy
closed	protect
disinfection	

1. Semipermanent lashes can last for up to _____ months with the right combination of products, adhesive, and proper application.

2. Contraindications to lash extensions are _____ eye irritations, eye allergies, blepharitis, glaucoma, excessive tearing, and thyroid problems.

3. When applying lashes, you should follow all sterilization and _____ guidelines.

4. If adhesive should get in the eye, immediately _____ with plenty of water and contact a physician.

5. The client's eyes should remain _____ during the entire procedure and at no time should adhesive be allowed to enter the eye.

6. The main purpose of the eyelash and eyelid is to _____ the eye from harmful substances or objects.

7. The three stages in a life cycle of a hair are anagen, _____ and telogen.

8. The use of as many _____ as possible will speed up your clean-up and minimize the sterilization process.

9. Three different types of looks can be accomplished by applying different lengths of lashes. For a natural look you would select lashes that are ¼ longer than the client's

lashes. For a feminine look, select lashes that are _____ longer than the client's lashes, and for a dramatic look, select lashes ½ again as long as the client's lashes.

10. Look for the following terms in the word search puzzle below.

adhesive	lash comb
cotton swab	micro swab
disposable	tweezers
eye makeup remover	under-eye pad
headband	

```
W  R  K  M  Z  E  C  O  I  K  V  F  W  H  R  L  L  N  G  J
K  B  M  R  R  T  L  Y  G  L  J  G  P  I  R  B  B  N  H  S
X  N  A  Z  W  S  C  C  F  I  C  I  T  W  F  C  B  L  U  B
I  G  R  Z  F  B  C  O  T  T  O  N  S  W  A  B  H  M  J  D
Q  U  S  B  J  U  N  R  J  T  J  P  N  M  L  Q  G  O  U  T
F  F  A  D  H  E  S  I  V  E  D  K  W  I  R  I  M  V  I  U
Y  F  W  E  L  W  Z  E  Q  N  Z  T  F  C  O  W  M  O  W  D
M  D  Q  C  L  W  Y  Q  O  M  T  G  O  R  T  F  Z  D  D  E
P  E  Y  E  M  A  K  E  U  P  R  E  M  O  V  E  R  I  T  U
D  D  I  Y  Q  E  Y  H  B  T  G  W  S  G  G  S  S  V  E
R  G  L  O  P  P  M  M  Q  S  R  L  I  W  A  F  F  P  N  X
U  E  N  K  I  D  O  H  F  G  W  G  I  A  M  D  O  O  Q  J
L  Y  R  Z  G  C  Y  P  W  H  D  L  S  B  H  L  E  S  O  P
K  Z  D  F  H  O  A  P  C  C  Z  R  J  N  H  Z  V  A  F  P
R  M  E  S  D  Z  W  T  R  K  E  N  A  G  I  C  U  B  R  I
Z  N  A  W  P  B  P  K  N  Z  Q  H  C  F  S  P  J  L  N  M
G  L  L  U  N  D  E  R  E  Y  E  P  A  D  S  U  C  E  P  B
O  E  I  J  W  C  T  E  Q  O  S  E  J  E  L  J  V  Q  P  K
D  P  I  S  V  H  W  J  W  A  G  N  T  R  B  D  W  Z  N  M
J  A  B  G  O  T  R  J  A  C  J  H  E  A  D  B  A  N  D  C
```

TECHNIQUE VARIATIONS

Answer the following questions.

1. For a larger, more open eye look you can:

   a. _____

   b. _____

   c. _____

2. To create a thick, lush, glamour look:

   a. _____

   b. _____

HOME-CARE INSTRUCTIONS

List the post-application instructions for the client.

1. _____
   _____

2. _____

3. _____
   _____

4. _____

5. _____
   _____

6. _____
   _____

COMMON REASONS LASH EXTENSIONS FALL OFF

1. List the common reasons lash extensions fall off.

   a. _____

   _____

   b. _____

   c. _____

   d. _____

EYELASH PERMING

Answer the following questions.

1. What two other services can you offer for eyelashes?

   a. _____

   b. _____

2. What is the purpose of perming eyelashes?

   _____

   _____

3. How long should you wait to apply eyelash extensions after perming the eyelashes?

   _____

4. How long should you wait to tint eyelashes after perming them? _____

EYELASH PERMING PROCEDURE

Find the following terms in the word search puzzle below.

applicator   hand mirror
clean towel   perming lotion
cotton swab   timer
glue   warm water

```
M  R  N  Y  F  E  T  L  R  J  R  R  T  F  D  A  Z  S  Y  B
V  Y  O  P  C  Z  N  B  U  P  D  K  M  P  R  W  Y  U  X  U
U  R  K  T  A  S  P  A  P  G  H  J  F  E  O  K  R  U  V  I
H  N  I  D  A  M  E  W  J  G  C  A  B  R  R  G  T  C  E  X
G  S  O  J  W  C  O  G  B  H  X  M  P  M  R  S  P  L  S  Z
V  B  T  M  E  T  I  J  T  D  I  R  I  I  I  W  Q  T  C  H
W  L  P  Q  V  U  X  L  I  Q  P  S  I  N  M  J  V  M  I  R
N  E  Y  C  O  P  L  K  P  P  D  A  V  G  D  W  Q  G  B  C
A  U  C  J  T  V  W  G  R  P  C  U  U  L  N  F  Z  A  M  L
G  J  C  L  Z  H  C  F  U  S  A  K  Z  O  A  E  W  U  R  H
J  T  E  T  E  L  L  F  K  A  F  E  W  T  H  S  E  D  H  T
A  E  W  H  O  A  Y  K  X  T  L  N  Y  I  N  G  Y  G  M  J
L  T  C  A  K  F  N  Z  W  T  I  J  Z  O  H  Q  Z  S  Z  D
O  J  R  L  R  H  Y  T  T  N  W  M  T  N  D  B  Z  J  P  V
M  L  H  D  S  M  L  Q  O  V  J  T  E  H  L  J  U  O  U  O
N  J  M  C  H  O  W  E  F  W  O  D  N  R  K  A  L  E  M  J
K  G  V  P  D  U  J  A  H  C  E  O  O  B  G  X  M  O  I  M
D  F  X  B  A  T  I  H  T  Y  C  L  C  K  L  L  A  X  A  F
R  A  E  X  G  M  A  F  H  E  D  Y  S  M  E  K  O  A  D  A
Z  K  O  C  W  P  W  F  S  U  R  V  I  K  E  C  Y  E  G  N
```

Fill in the missing steps in the following procedure.

1. Select the roller: smaller rollers, medium rollers, and large rollers.

2. Cleanse the eyelashes, removing all eye makeup.

3. _____

4. The rollers are self-adhesive so be careful to handle them only at the tips. Bend the roller slightly to fit the shape of the eyelid and trim the rod to the appropriate length of the eyelid.

5. Apply eyelash perming glue in a line at the base of the lashes and position the roller as close as possible to the root of the lashes. After positioning the roller, add more glue on the top of the roller.

6. _____

_____

7. Apply perm solution with a cotton swab or manufacturer's applicator across the lashes adhered to the rod. Avoid contact with the skin. Carefully follow manufacturer's instructions; depending on the kit, timing ranges anywhere from 8 to 15 minutes.

8. _____

_____

_____

9. Apply setting or neutralizer lotion to lashes with application stick. Leave neutralizer on according to manufacturer's instructions, generally 5 to 10 minutes.

10. _____

11. If the kit includes a post-treatment lotion, apply it on an applicator stick or cotton swab. Let lotion set for 5 minutes or according to manufacturer's instruction.

12. _____

_____

_____

13. Clean lashes with a warm, damp cloth.

MINERAL MAKEUP

Answer the following questions by using the words from the word bank.

70% to 90%	excellent	mica
1994	facial spritz	minerals
bismusth oxychloride	fine lines	slip and glide
boron nitrides	inert	sunscreen
breathe and function	iron oxide	weightless
chemical sunscreen	jawline	zinc oxide
dimethicone	kabuki	

1. When was the term coined to describe a concentrated pigment powder that was unlike the widely used, predominantly talc-based formulae found throughout the cosmetic world? _____

2. Traditionally, color cosmetics—base, blush and eye shadows—contain _____ talcum powder.

3. Some of the mineral makeup usually comprises a selection of the following minerals: titanium dioxide, zinc oxide, _____ bismuth oxychloride, boron nitride and iron oxides.

4. Minerals used in powders are inert substances. _____ is defined as something that cannot support bacterial life.

5. Titanium dioxide is one of two ingredients approved by the FDA as a physical _____

6. _____ is commonly used as a coating to increase the light-scattering properties of TiO_2.

7. _____ is approved by the FDA as a physical sunscreen.

8. Mica gives _____ to the finished product.

9. _____ is a synthetically prepared iridescent white or nearly white powder.

10. _____ is a white, silky powder that gives smoothness, coverage, slip, and sheen to the finished product.

11. _____ commonly known as rust, is primarily used as a colorant.

12. Mineral makeup gives _____ coverage with very little product.

13. When applied to clean, moisturized skin, these particles cling together and create a surface tension that overcomes gravity and holds the _____ tightly to the skin.

14. Minerals allow the skin to _____ normally.

15. A mineral makeup with an SPF can eliminate the need for _____

16. If minerals are applied properly, they should feel _____ on the skin.

17. Foundation that is too dark will exaggerate _____ and accentuate pores.

18. To test the foundation color correctly, you should test it on your _____

19. The best tool for loose mineral powder is a _____ brush.

20. If the minerals look powdery, wait a few minutes for the skin's natural oils to emerge or you may speed the process by using a _____

APPLYING MINERAL MAKEUP

Find the following terms in the word search puzzle on the following page.

brushes	moisturizer
cleanser	tissues
drape	towel
gloves	sponges
mineral powders	

```
J U P W B L X Y V T K Z K A X G K O J L
C V X T I S S U E S H H V F E I I J A P
Q S N V O T I G F P Y F K S A Z I R O J
K C V X H Z V J Z Z T E E Z S R O Y O W
S S E O R N P W M H Y O V F E E M G H O
Q U E J G V E E S D Z T W S Q H O D V F
B X U J X Z D D Q K Q H N E L Y I X U B
O L Q Y Y A M F I F S A K V L J S K V P
B F Y S E G N O P S E L U C X T T P P I
X M Q S C U M T Y L D Q M T C I U D P W
V K H T N Z Y C C A G T E B G D R Q A A
S Z U Y S R E D W O P L A R E N I M L P
Y M C N N H Q Z Y T U T N W V E Z A N K
T K S E V O L G N C U C T P G P E V I W
G U R G G N M Q L O A N O I F H R L D N
O K V K Z J W S C I U Q T V E N O Y Z I
Z B C Q F U F B A P X J V P F J T S S O
I B S E H S U R B C Y P A V X D P X U Q
Y N E A X L D N Y R P R Q U R C T E L O
F O X Z O B R E R U D Y G F H U M X T B
```

PROCEDURE FOR APPLYING MINERAL MAKEUP

Fill in the missing steps within the procedure.

1. Pre-cleanse client's skin and pat dry.

2. Apply moisturizer.

3. _____

4. Dispense some of the minerals onto a working pallet.

5. _____

6. Divide the client's face into quadrants, starting with the forehead. Apply one brushload to each quadrant. Do not apply too heavily; light coats are best.

7. _____

8. If additional coverage is required, apply thin additional coats.

APPLICATION PROBLEMS

List and explain three application problems.

1. _____

   _____

   _____

   _____

2. _____

   _____

   _____

3. _____

   _____

   _____

MINERALS FOR CAMOUFLAGE

Answer the following questions.

1. Even though green has been used for a long time in the makeup world to cover redness, _____ is all you need to neutralize red in the skin.

2. How should circles under the eyes be concealed?

   _____

   _____

3. What are some of the reasons someone can get dark circles under the eyes?

   a. _____

   b. _____

   c. _____

   d. _____

e. _____

f. _____

g. _____

4. What are the two types of mineral under-eye concealer? _____

5. Cream mineral under-eye concealers usually come in a variety of _____ tones.

6. Yellow will be your best friend for covering the _____ in bruises and tattoos.

7. To conceal yellow bruising, using a _____ concealer can often be helpful. Simplify the process by using a _____ mineral powder.

AIRBRUSH MAKEUP

1. What size airbrush nozzles should be used during the following procedures?

   a. Airbrushing Beauty Makeup   _____

   b. Airbrushing Body Makeup   _____

   c. Airbrush Tanning   _____

2. What are the two actions you can take using a dual-action airbrush?

   _____

   _____

3. How do you accomplish a narrow spray pattern?

   _____

   _____

   _____

   _____

4. How do you accomplish a wide spray pattern?

   _____

   _____

   _____

   _____

5. How often should an airbrush be cleaned?

   _____

MAXIMUM COVERAGE MAKEUP

Unscramble this list of materials and implements.

riarsubh teeqpimun

irasuhbr daonufoinst

dpsioalseb ogensp

etstgni wdpreo

repad

dnehbada

posisaldeb upc

tsreifk

levgos

MAXIMUM COVERAGE MAKEUP PROCEDURE

Fill in the missing steps within the procedure.

Preparation

1. Prepare the work area for makeup application.

2. _____

3. Gather supplies.

4. Review the client's history with her and have her read and sign a consent form.

5. Review the client's expectations and the procedure

Procedure

1. Seat and drape the client. Protect her hair, if appropriate.

2. _____

3. Select a foundation color that matches the primary skin tone that surrounds the discoloration. Keep this color aside. You will use it for the final layer.

4. _____

5. Use the neutralizing color with a light touch targeting the natural shape of the hyperpigmentation or the design of the tattoo.

a. _____

b. _____

c. Repeat these two steps to achieve coverage.

d. _____
_____

e. Rinse the airbrush cup to clean foundation from it.

6. When you've achieved 90% coverage and neutralization.

a. _____

b. Now introduce the primary skin tone shade selected in step 1.

c. _____

7. If the skin's surface has freckles, you will need to reintroduce them.

8. Create a stencil with frisket film. It can be pierced with a pin to create odd-shaped holes, recreating freckles.

9. _____

PERMANENT COSMETICS

Use the terms in the word bank to fill in answers for the questions below.

advanced	medical condition
estheticians	rotary
eyeliner	single
hands-on	tattooing

1. The Society of Permanent Cosmetic Professionals (SPCP) Vision 2006 study results show that 36% of all permanent cosmetic technicians are also _____

2. In 2006 the governor of Oklahoma signed a bill legalizing _____ and permanent cosmetics so that it is now recognized and legal throughout the United States.

3. Those wanting to learn permanent cosmetics should recognize this is a skill that can only be achieved with _____ training and lots of practice.

4. A fundamental training is in eyebrows, _____ and an introduction to lip-liner.

5. Full lip color is considered an _____ procedure, as is areola repigmentation, cheek color, eye shadow, or scar camouflage.

6. The common types of equipment include the manual method, _____ and coil.

7. If the client has a _____ that could impact the healing process, she would be directed to consult her physician and obtain a medical release before the procedure is performed.

8. Regardless of the equipment or device being used for the permanent makeup process, needles and pigments are considered _____ use.

21 SPA TREATMENTS

Date: _____

Rating: _____

Text Pages: 563–599

UNDERSTANDING SPAS AND THEIR SERVICES

Answer the following questions.

1. How many types of spas are there? _____ Describe each below.

2. Day spa: _____
   _____
   _____
   _____
   _____

3. Destination spa: _____
   _____
   _____
   _____
   _____
   _____
   _____

4. Resort spa: _____
   _____
   _____
   _____

5. Medical spa: _____
   _____
   _____
   _____
   _____
   _____
   _____
   _____
   _____

_____

_____

_____

6. Fitness/health clubs: _____

_____

_____

_____

_____

_____

_____

_____

_____

7. Hospitals and rehabilitation facilities: _____

_____

_____

_____

8. Wellness centers: _____

_____

_____

_____

_____

_____

9. What types of tables are used for body treatments?

_____

10. Describe a wet table. _____

_____

_____

_____

_____

12. What is the HIPAA law?

_____

13. What information do you need to obtain prior to giving a body treatment service?

_____

14. List the contradictions for a body treatment.

    a. _____

    b. _____

c. _____

d. _____

e. _____

f. _____

g. _____

h. _____

i. _____

j. _____

k. _____

l. _____

m. _____

n. _____

o. _____

p. _____

15. List the steps for the table setup.

a. _____

b. _____

c. _____

d. _____
_____

e. _____
_____

f. _____

g. _____

16. What should you tell your client to make him or her more comfortable?

_____

17. List the Client Preparation Procedures:

a. _____
_____

b. _____

c. _____

d. _____

18. What are some steps that can ensure your client's comfort?

a. _____

b. _____

c. _____

d. _____

e. _____

f. _____

19. Fill in the missing words in the following paragraph using words from the word bank below.

foils	showers
injuries	tepid
plastic	treatment

Help clients off of the _____ table slowly to avoid _____, as they may be unsteady after lying down for an extended period of time. During some treatments, you may escort or help your client into the shower. Before a client _____, check the water _____, setting it to cool, then _____ to help slowly lower his or her body temperature. If your treatment involves the use of _____ or _____, remove these and re-drape the client so that they do not slip and fall from the materials.

20. How should a body product be removed with hot towels?

_____
_____
_____
_____
_____
_____
_____
_____
_____
_____
_____

PROCEDURE FOR A BODY SCRUB WITH HYDRATING PACK/MASK

Fill in the missing steps for the body scrub and hydrating pack/mask procedure.

Preparation

1. Prepare the table with the materials you will need; remember that the outermost layer of material represents the first treatment.

2. _____

3. Prepare hot, wet towels and place them in the towel cabinet.

4. Review client health history to ensure that the client is still a candidate for this treatment.

5. _____
   _____

6. _____

Procedure

1. Prepare the body with a cleansing gel or lotion, depending on the client's skin type.

   a. Use light effleurage movements over the entire body.

   b. _____

2. Spray appropriate toner with the Lucas or other spray applicator of your choice.

3. _____

   a. _____

   b. For enhanced exfoliation, use a handheld or machine-aided brush.

c. _____
_____
_____
_____
_____
_____

d. If a granular scrub is used, rinse with large, wet sponges or hot, moist towels. Remember to maintain proper draping, exposing only the area being worked on.

4. As in step 2, spray appropriate toner with the Lucas spray applicator of your choice.

5. _____
_____
_____

_____ If working on the back of the body, take this time to do a scalp massage. If doing the front of the body, use this time to give the client a hand or foot massage or treatment.

6. _____
_____

7. _____

8. Help the client turn over, maintaining the appropriate draping protocols. Repeat this entire process on the other side of the body.

Post-procedure

1. Help the client get up off the bed carefully.

2. _____

Clean-up and Disinfection

1. Follow clean-up and disinfection procedures in accordance with state guidelines.

2. _____

COMMON INGREDIENTS USED IN BODY TREATMENTS

Match the ingredients with their definitions.

alpha hydroxy acid   Used to boost collagen synthesis

beta hydroxy acid   Skin exfoliant

caffeine   Also called China clay

collagen   Moisturizer that has conditioning properties

green tea extract	Also known as "cyclic acid"
hyaluronic acid	Is added to topical creams for its moisturizing benefits
kaolin	Has the ability to kill bacteria
shea butter	Contains "catechins"
sulfur	A stimulant
vitamin C	An example would be salicylic acid

SEAWEED WRAPS

Answer the following questions.

1. What benefits does a cocoon wrap offer?

    _____

    _____

2. What are the benefits of a seaweed wrap?

    _____

3. During a seaweed wrap, how is the body exfoliated before the algae is applied?

    _____

PROCEDURE FOR APPLYING AND REMOVING A SEAWEED WRAP

Fill in the missing steps in the following procedure.

Preparation

1. Prepare the treatment table with a protective covering (such as a sheet, plastic protector sheet, wool blanket, cellophane sheet, or space blanket, and a top sheet or towel).

2. _____

    _____

3. Review client health history to ensure that the client is still a candidate for this treatment.

4. _____

5. _____

    _____

    _____

6. Pre-treat the client by cleansing and toning the skin, one area at a time prior to masking.

7. _____

Procedure

1. If the client is female, instruct her to cross her arms (to hold the modesty towel into place), and assist her into a seated position.

2. _____
   _____

3. _____

4. _____

5. Apply the mixture to the legs and buttocks starting with the nearest leg. This is accomplished by gently raising the knees and applying the mixture to the backs of the legs to the buttocks.

6. _____

7. Pull the plastic drape across the leg over the mud, and reposition the towel.

8. _____

9. _____

10. Next fold up the layers or blankets onto the client. Use a towel around the neck to prevent heat loss. Process for the desired time, which is usually 25 minutes.

11. _____
    _____
    _____

12. Starting with the nearest leg, remove all product from front of the leg. Raise the knee to allow complete removal of product from the back of the leg. Shift the plastic out of the way and re-cover client with a clean towel.

13. Repeat this process with the opposite leg. To remove the plastic out from under the client, shift it as far as possible to the left side and have the client elevate his or her hips slightly to assist you. Slide the plastic completely from under the client's lower body, ensure that all product has been removed, and re-cover the client.

14. _____

15. _____

16. Apply the lotion to the opposite leg.

17. _____
    _____

18. Apply lotion to the client's chest and arms. The stomach is optional.

19. _____

20. Remove the last of the plastic.

21. _____
_____
_____

Post-procedure

1. _____

2. _____

Clean-up and Disinfection

1. Follow clean-up and disinfection procedures in accordance with state guidelines.

2. _____

HERBAL WRAPS

Answer the following questions.

1. What are the Ace® bandages soaked in?

_____

2. What benefits do the herbs offer?

_____
_____

3. What is the definition for diaphoretic?

_____

4. What is a hydrocollator?

_____

PROCEDURE FOR A BODY WRAP

Fill in the missing steps for the procedure for a body wrap.

Preparation

1. Prepare the moist heat unit following manufacturer's directions. The suggested temperature range is 150°F to 185°F.

2. _____

_____

3. _____

_____

4. _____

_____

5. Set up the treatment room in standard spa treatment manner, from the treatement bed outward:

   a. Water protective cover

   b. Wool blanket

   c. Metallic spa sheet

   d. Body Pack film (Optional)

   e. Large bath towel (for dry brushing step)

   f. Spa towel across the head of the lounge

6. Review client health history to ensure that the client is still a candidate for this treatment.

7. _____

_____

8. Some technicians offer the client warm herbal tea to raise core body temperature. Alternatively, a client can take a shower or sit in the sauna.

9. _____

_____

_____

Procedure

1. _____

_____

_____

2. Assist the client back up from the bed, keeping him or her draped in a large bath sheet if nude.

3. _____

_____

_____

_____

_____

_____

4. Assist the client back onto the bed lying faceup on the sheet.

5. Quickly wrap the linen sheet around the client's entire body. (You can also layer the sheet.)

6. _____

    _____

    _____

7. Wrap the thermal blanket over the herbal wrap sheet.

8. Wrap the insulating blanket over the thermal blanket.

9. Wrap the wool blanket over the thermal blanket.

10. _____

    a. _____

    b. _____

    c. _____

11. Apply a cool, folded washcloth to the client's forehead and across the eyes. For additional comfort, you can place a pillow under his or her head. If the client gets too warm, open the blanket around the neck.

12. Leave the client wrapped for 20 to 30 minutes. During this time, perform a scalp massage or play soothing music.

13. After the wrap has processed, remove the layers slowly, allowing the client to get acclimated to the cooler temperature of the room.

14. _____

15. _____

    _____

16. As this is a detoxifying treatment, no lotions should be applied.

17. Allow the client to lie back down and rest, if desired.

Post-procedure

1. Offer the client water to rehydrate.

2. _____
    _____

3. _____

Clean-up and Disinfection

1. _____

2. Disinfect any implements following state guidelines.

3. Clean and disinfect the moist heat unit following the manufacturer's directions.

HERBS USED IN WRAPS

Write the letter of each herb next to its beneficial quality.

A.	Allspice	_____ Astringent properties
B.	Burdock	_____ Soothing
C.	Sage	_____ Increase blood circulation
D.	Comfrey	_____ Astringent; toning; stimulating
E.	Eucalyptus	_____ Muscle relaxant
F.	Basil	_____ Increases circulation; detoxifying agent
G.	Clove	_____ Stimulating
H.	Rosemary	_____ Soothing
I.	Lavender	_____ Effective with arthritis
J.	Ginger	_____ Relieves bruises and inflammation

WRAPPING AGENTS

Answer the following questions.

1. What purpose does a cellophane body wrap serve?

    _____
    _____

2. What purpose does a blanket wrap serve?

_____

3. What purpose does a Kneipp body wrap serve?

_____

_____

_____

SOOTHING LEG TREATMENT

Fill in the missing steps in the following procedure.

Preparation

1. Prepare the treatment table with bottom linens and blankets.

2. _____

_____

3. Place a small plastic covering on top of this towel.

4. _____

5. _____

_____

6. Review client health history to ensure that the client is still a candidate for this treatment.

7. Tell the client what to expect during the treatment.

8. _____

_____

Procedure

1. _____

_____

_____

2. Now on the moist skin, begin applying a mixture or mineral water, fango mud, and exfoliating granules.

   a. _____

   _____

   b. _____

3. Using the same steps as above, remove the product thoroughly with warm, moist towels that have been soaked in mineral water and warmed in towel cabinet.

   a. _____

   _____

   b. _____

4. Repeat this process for the left leg. As you remove product from this leg, slide the plastic drape from under the client and remove. The client is now laying on the towel on top of the second sheet of plastic.

5. _____

   _____

6. _____

7. Slide towel out from beneath client's legs so he or she is against the plastic. Using a large brush or your hands, layer fango mud onto right leg front and back.

   a. _____

   _____

   b. _____

8. Repeat this process on the other leg.

9. Cover client's legs with blankets to keep them warm. Leave mud in place for 20 minutes.

10. _____

11. _____

12. Repeat for left leg. Allow client to rest.

13. Starting with the right leg, remove mud completely. Rinse well and wipe with a warm, wet towel. Cover the client with the towel when complete.

14. Repeat the removal procedure on the left leg.

15. _____

   _____

16. Repeat on the left leg.

Optional: If your license permits, you may finish with a drainage massage or employ pressotherapy.

Post-procedure

1. Offer the client water to rehydrate her.

2. Inform her of any specific post-treatment instructions.

Clean-up and Disinfection

1. _____

2. Disinfect any implements following state guidelines.

HYDROTHERAPY AND OTHER SPECIALTY TREATMENTS

Answer the following questions.

1. What is the first step to beginning a shower treatment?

   _____

2. What should the water temperature be?

   _____

3. What is a scotch hose?

   _____

4. What should the temperature of the water be during a scotch hose treatment?

   _____

5. What types of "baths" are available in some resort spas?

   _____

6. Describe raindrop therapy.

   _____
   _____
   _____
   _____

7. Describe music therapy.

   _____

8. List the benefits of music therapy

   a. _____
      _____
      _____

   b. _____
      _____

   c. _____
      _____

   d. _____
      _____

e. _____

_____

f. _____

_____

g. _____

_____

_____

h. _____

_____

i. _____

_____

_____

j. _____

_____

_____

k. _____

_____

l. _____

22 ALTERNATIVE THERAPIES

Date: _____

Rating: _____

Text Pages: 600–626

THE HISTORY OF ALTERNATIVE MEDICINE

Use the terms in the word bank to fill out the questions below.

aura	Kirlian cameras
balance	man
chakra	medicine
compassion	nature
energy	vibration
interchangeable	

1. What we now call Complementary and Alternative Medicine (CAM) was once the only

    _____

2. Famous physicist Albert Einstein recognized this separation between nature and
    _____ as creating a prison.

3. Einstein said that the only way to free ourselves from this prison was by "widening our
    circle of _____ to embrace all living creatures, the whole of nature and its beauty."

ENERGY BASICS

1. The spirit of man, _____, and the universe are one and the same.

2. If someone is out of balance, nature can fill the void and restore the _____.

3. Everything has _____, whether it is a person, animal, or objects. Within this
    energy field is a _____, or frequency, that includes specific characteristics innate
    to that energy.

4. Spirit, energy body, or essence are _____ terms describing the life force
    energy of all living things.

5. The inner face is the subtle energy body that we refer to as the _____ *system.*

6. _____ invented by a Russian couple Semyon and Valentine Kirlian in the 1930s, are used to photograph the colors of the aura so that people without psychic vision are able to see the energy of the chakras made visible.

7. Describe an aura.

_____

ENERGY MANAGEMENT

Answer the following questions.

1. What is Leaky Aura Syndrome?

_____

_____

2. Explain energy management.

_____

_____

3. What are some of the things that can throw off your balance energetically?

a. _____

b. _____

c. _____

d. _____

e. _____

f. _____

THE FOUR ENERGY BODIES

Answer the following questions.

1. What is the mental body?

_____

_____

2. What is the emotional body? _____

3. What is the spirit or energy body?

_____

4. Fill in the missing information in the chart.

The Four Intelligences as They Relate to the Physical, Mental, Emotional and Spirit/Energy Bodies		
Sensory Intelligence	Physical Body	
Cognitive Intelligence		
Feeling Intelligence	Emotional Body	
Intuitive Intelligence		

KEEPING THE ENERGY BODIES IN BALANCE

Answer the following questions.

1. Define aromatherapy.

_____

_____

_____

2. List the aromas that have the benefits shown.
    Calms the emotions: _____
    Lifts the spirits: _____
    Enhances mental clarity and focus: _____

3. List the following herbs by their benefits:
    Lifts the spirits: _____
    Calms the emotions: _____
    Enhances mental clarity, better memory recall: _____
    _____

MINI-MEDITATION AND BREATHING EXERCISE

Answer the following questions.

1. What are the benefits of controlled breathing?
    _____

2. When performing deep breathing, think of what you would like more of and breathe in that quality. What thoughts should you exhale?

    a. Breathe in Acceptance and breathe out _____

    b. Breathe in Confidence and breathe out _____

    c. Breathe in Gratitude and breathe out _____

    d. Breathe in Abundance and breathe out _____

    e. Breathe in Peacefulness and breathe out _____

    f. Breathe in Love and breathe out _____

    g. Breathe in Awareness and breathe out _____

THE CHAKRA SYSTEM

Answer the following questions.

1. What does the word *chakra* originate from?
    _____

2. What is each chakra associated with?
    _____
    _____

3. Use the words in the word bank to complete the paragraph below.

chakras   life
create   place
heart   Reiki
intuitive

_____ 4 through 7 are connected to spiritual development on a more conscious level. Operating through the upper chakras, you have use of all of your intelligences—feeling, _____, sensory, and cognitive. You have connection to your _____, voice, vision and intuitive insight to _____ your life rather than react to it. You receive information from a higher source, have a clear vision of the big picture and how you fit into the picture, and you are able to speak clearly about your vision from the heart. When you come from this _____, you feel at peace and comfortable in your own skin and environment and you are able to feel a sense of purpose and passion for _____.

REIKI HANDS-ON HEALING

1. What is Reiki?

   _____

   _____

2. What does *Rei* mean? _____

3. What does *Ki* mean? _____

4. Who developed Reiki? _____

5. List the benefits of Reiki.

   a. _____

   b. _____

   c. _____

       _____

   d. _____

       _____

   e. _____

   f. _____

   g. _____

h. _____

i. _____

j. _____

k. _____

6. Explain what type of healing each Reiki class offers:

First Degree: _____

Second Degree: _____

Third Degree: _____

BACH FLOWER REMEDIES

Answer the following questions.

1. Who developed the Bach Flower Essences? _____

2. How many flower essences were developed first? _____

3. List the benefits of each Bach Flower Remedy.

   a. White Chestnut _____

   b. Walnut _____

   c. Larch _____

Rock water _____
_____

Vervain _____

Holly _____

Rescue remedy
essence and cream _____

POPULAR HEALING STONES

Answer the following questions.

1. What are healing stones?

_____

2. What are the four different types of stones?

   a. Warm stones are _____.

   b. Muted stones are _____.

   c. Cool stones are _____.

   d. Cleansing stones are _____.

3. Each color has its own frequency or _____.

4. If you add white to a color, it is a _____.

5. If you add black to a color, it is a _____.

6. Colors opposite each other on the color wheel are called _____.

7. Placing a complementary color on a chakra will _____.

8. What is the contraindication of a red stone? _____

9. List the steps to sanitize and clear your stones.

   a. _____
   _____
   _____

   b. _____
   _____

   c. _____
   _____

   • _____
   _____

   • _____
   _____

STONES AND CHAKRAS

List the stones for each chakra and explain what benefit each gas.

First Chakra _____
_____

First Chakra _____

_____

_____

Second Chakra _____

_____

_____

Third Chakra _____

_____

_____

Fourth Chakra _____

_____

_____

Fifth Chakra _____

_____

_____

Fifth Chakra _____

_____

Fifth Chakra _____

_____

_____

_____

Sixth Chakra _____

_____

_____

_____

Fourth and Seventh Chakra _____

_____

_____

_____

Seventh Chakra _____

_____

_____

AN ALTERNATIVE THERAPIES WORD SEARCH

Find the following terms in the word search puzzle below.

balance	gemstone
chakra	leaky aura
citrine	mental
color	Reiki
energy body	soul

```
I  X  W  G  X  A  Q  M  C  A  B  X  A  S  J  M  R  I  T  P
N  F  J  G  I  R  E  D  Q  P  V  Q  O  T  E  A  R  F  L  X
P  V  O  Z  M  N  T  X  Y  P  N  U  Q  N  F  E  T  A  M  A
S  T  M  P  F  O  O  A  R  N  L  J  T  G  S  B  S  E  F  Z
A  L  A  K  B  W  W  A  C  B  Q  A  J  Q  W  P  N  Y  R  V
Q  L  T  Y  P  V  Y  O  Q  C  L  W  E  W  R  O  P  X  I  G
B  R  M  I  T  Z  Z  S  L  Z  K  M  S  A  T  R  M  A  G  Q
M  E  Z  Z  W  U  Q  U  P  Y  S  B  Z  S  Q  V  R  H  X  Z
X  N  Z  C  T  R  E  I  K  I  Q  F  M  E  H  K  A  K  T  P
B  I  Q  H  F  J  C  G  P  W  C  E  H  D  A  I  Y  H  J  O
C  R  V  G  W  W  C  V  E  L  G  W  K  H  X  D  T  E  N  Z
W  T  J  R  B  Z  N  H  E  V  Z  N  C  P  O  C  R  R  V  X
L  I  W  O  F  R  N  F  T  G  O  Y  Y  B  M  U  B  C  Y  O
E  C  Y  L  K  S  L  P  P  Y  J  L  Y  J  Q  X  C  D  V  B
W  L  Y  O  M  P  W  F  C  K  F  G  V  D  M  W  S  L  J  D
S  S  M  C  P  K  M  Y  I  A  R  U  A  Y  K  A  E  L  E  P
J  K  L  L  J  U  K  R  Y  E  I  L  K  O  D  V  L  Q  X  W
L  A  S  O  G  K  E  O  N  C  I  I  N  P  R  Y  E  P  A  T
E  C  N  A  L  A  B  E  V  J  L  J  L  Q  U  N  S  A  U  X
V  G  U  V  B  Z  Q  V  Y  Z  A  A  P  U  J  V  L  Z  L  D
```

23 AYURVEDA THEORY AND TREATMENTS

Date: _____

Rating: _____

Text Pages: 627–659

WHAT ARE AYURVEDIC TREATMENTS? _____

Answer the following questions.

1. What does Ayurveda refer to? _____
   _____
   _____

2. Use the terms in the word bank to complete the paragraphs below.

acupuncture	kinesiology
astrology	mother of all healing
aromatherapy	unconditional
foot reflexology	sound therapy

"Ayurveda is sometimes called the "_____" because the treatments demonstrate the finest qualities of a mother—love and respect for each and every client, gentleness, understanding and _____ support. It is the source of many types of body care used today, including _____ polarity therapy, full-body oil massage, deep tissue massage, _____ physiotherapy, _____ and hydrotherapy. It also gave birth to modern medical treatments such as nutrition, herbal supplementation, homeopathy, _____ psychiatry, and surgery, including cosmetic surgery.

Ayurveda provides care and wisdom from every available source, including more esoteric studies such as _____; mantra or healing through prayer and chanting; color therapy; music or _____; gem therapy and the use of stones; and alchemical preparations."

3. Explain the five Vedic principles.

   a. Sound: _____
      _____
      _____

   b. Sight: _____
      _____
      _____

c.   Smell: _____

_____

_____

d.   Touch: _____

_____

_____

e.   Taste: _____

_____

_____

_____

f.   Heart Feeling: _____

_____

_____

4.   What is the combination of subtle energies or five great elements called?

_____

THE DOSHAS

1.   Describe the three doshas:

a.   Vata: _____

_____

_____

_____

_____

_____

b.   Pitta: _____

_____

_____

_____

_____

_____

_____

c.   Kapha: _____

_____

_____

_____

_____

2. What does Prakuti mean? _____

3. What does Vikruti mean? _____

THE QUALITIES OF THE FIVE ELEMENTS

1. Explain the qualities of the five elements.

Space: _____

Air: _____

Fire: _____

Water: _____

Earth: _____

2. If one element is allowed to accumulate, then problems will eventually manifest. What problems happen if there is:

Extra earth: cellulite

Extra water: _____

Extra fire: _____

Extra air: _____

Extra space: _____

VATA BODY-MIND CHARACTERISTICS

Answer the following questions.

1. The Vata body will appear as _____

2. The Vata actions will be _____

3.   The Vata will talk about _____

4.   What unbalances the Vata dosha? _____
_____
_____
_____

5.   What can be done to balance the Vata dosha? _____
_____
_____

6.   What are the key words to help customize a treatment for a Vata dosha? _____
_____

7.   What treatments would be the best for the Vata dosha? _____
_____

PITTA BODY-MIND CHARACTERISTICS

Answer the following questions.

1.   The Pitta body will appear as _____

2.   The Pitta actions will be _____

3.   The Pitta's speech will be _____

4.   What unbalances the Pitta dosha? _____
_____
_____

5.   What can be done to balance the Pitta dosha? _____
_____

6.   What are the key words to help customize a treatment for a Pitta dosha? _____
_____

7.   What treatments would be best for the Pitta dosha? _____
_____
_____
_____

KAPHA BODY-MIND CHARACTERISTICS

Answer the following questions.

1. The Kapha body will appear as _____
   _____

2. The Kapha actions will be _____

3. The Kapha's speech will be _____

4. What unbalances the Kapha dosha? _____
   _____
   _____
   _____

5. What can be done to balance the Kapha dosha? _____
   _____

6. What are the key words to help customize a treatment for a Kapha dosha? _____
   _____

7. What treatments would be best for the Kapha dosha? _____
   _____

CUSTOMIZED ESSENTIAL OIL BLENDS AND HERBS

Describe the oil blends and herbs for each dosha.

1. Vata Blend: _____
   _____
   _____
   _____
   _____

2. Pitta Blend: _____
   _____
   _____
   _____
   _____
   _____

3. Kapha Blend: _____
   _____
   _____

_____

_____

MAGICAL MARMAS

Answer the following questions.

1.   What is a marma point? _____

2.   How many marma points are there? _____

3.   How does a marma point close? _____

BASIC MARMA POINT MASSAGE

Fill in the missing steps in the procedure below.

Preparation

1.   _____

2.   Gather supplies and products.

3.   Warm the oil in a massage oil heater or other warming device.

4.   Review the client's history with him or her and assure the appropriateness of the procedure. Then select the appropriate ayurvedic massage blend based on the client's dosha.

Procedure

1.   _____
     _____

2.   Position 2, on the midline of the head, 8 finger widths above the eyebrows. Using your thumb, middle finger, or fourth finger, perform 15 to 30 gentle clockwise circles.

3.   _____
     _____
     _____

4.   _____
     _____
     _____

5. Position 5. Place hands on both sides of the head at the top of the spine. Support the head with one hand and massage with the other, rotating your hands as needed to completely massage both sides of the head. Work deeply enough to manipulate the skin and muscles of the scalp. Use all of your finger tips to generally move over the scalp using sufficient pressure to gently move the scalp over the skull and systematically working over entire scalp.

6. _____
   _____
   _____

7. _____
   _____

8. Position 8, the side of neck, 4 finger widths below the earlobe. Apply gentle lymph drainage in a press-release pattern, repeating three times.

9. _____
   _____

10. _____
    _____

11. Position 11, mid-neck or around the Adam's Apple. Apply gentle clockwise circular massage, repeating three times.

12. Position 12, slightly behind the top of the breastbone. Apply gentle lymph drainage. Press and release gently towards the waist. Repeat three times.

13. _____

14. _____

15. _____

16. Position 16, halfway up the nose on either side. Press and release gently 10 times.

17. Position 17, in the outer corner of each eye. Press away from the eye toward the boney orbit. Press and release gently 10 times.

18. _____
    _____

19. _____

20. Position 20, in the hollows of both temples. Gently rub with 10 small circles.

21. Position 21, in the middle of the forehead. Gently rub in single clockwise spiral, starting very tiny and slowly expanding to cover entire middle of forehead.

22. Decant appropriate ayurvedic oil into palms of your hands but do not rub hands together.

23. _____

    _____

24. _____

    _____

    _____

    _____

25. Position 24. Chin to temple glide. Using two fingers of each hand, trace along the jawline from the center of the chin to the temple, and perform five circles on the temporal region.

26. _____

    a. _____

    b. _____

       _____

    c. _____

       _____

    d. _____

27. Position 26. Up the face movement using two fingers from each hand simultaneously.

    a. Perform three press-release patterns on the center of the mentalis.

    b. Glide to the corners of the mouth and perform five small circles.

    c. Glide to the underside of the masseter and perform three press-release patterns.

    d. Glide to the temples and perform five circles.

28. Position 27. Center of lip to mastoid (both hands simultaneously).

    a. _____

       _____

    b. _____

       _____

c. _____

d. Slide toward the ear and then up and over the ear to the mastoid process.

e. Perform five circles on the mastoid process.

29. **Position 28, nose to mastoid. This is done one side of the face at a time. The hand not being used for massage is resting on the top of the client's head.**

    a. At the flare of the right nostril, perform three press-release patterns.

    b. Stroke across the cheekbone to the ear, and then slide up and over to the mastoid process.

    c. Perform five circles on the mastoid process.

    d. Repeat on the left side of the face.

30. _____

    a. _____
       _____

    b. _____

    c. _____

31. _____
    _____
    _____

    a. Starting at the inner corner of the eye socket, perform three press-release patterns.

    b. Glide about a quarter of the way across the eye and repeat.

    c. Glide about half of the way across the eye, and repeat.

    d. Glide about three-quarters of the way across the eye, and repeat.

    e. Glide to outer corner of the eye and "jiggle" the tissue gently but firmly.

32. _____
    _____

    a. _____
       _____
       _____

b. _____

c. Glide a quarter of the way along the brow bone and repeat.

d. Glide halfway along brow bone and repeat.

e. Glide three-quarters of the way along brow bone and repeat.

f. _____

33. Position 32, brow pinch. This is done with the thumbs and index fingers of both hands at the same time.

   a. Starting at the inner corners of the brow, gently but firmly pinch and release.

   b. _____

   c. _____

34. Position 33, nose-forehead spiral

   a. _____
      _____

   b. _____
      _____

35. (Position 34, zigzags. This movement is a bit stimulating to slowly rouse the client.)

   a. _____
      _____

   b. Trace zigzags across forehead to one temple and then back across forehead to other temple.

36. Position 35. Next offer a more vigorous massage of the scalp and ears using pads of fingers or full hands, as best fits the client's head and your hand size.

37. _____
    _____
    _____

38. _____
    _____

39. Position 38. Complete with appropriate SPF product or move into additional facial steps as desired.

SHIRODHARA TREATMENT

Answer the following questions.

1.   Explain the Shirodhara treatment: _____

_____

2.   List the contraindications to the Shirodhara treatment.

    a. _____

    b. _____

    c. _____

    d. _____

    e. _____

    f. _____

    g. _____

    h. _____

    i. _____

    j. _____

24 WORKING IN A MEDICAL SETTING

Date:

Rating:

Text Pages: 661–671

INTRODUCTION

Find the following terms in the word search puzzle below.

anecdotal   control group   medical spa   plastic surgeon
board certified   cosmetic dermatology   placebo   scope of practice

```
I  D  B  P  N  Y  Y  X  Q  Q  C  A  I  O  H  N  W  G  D  W  J  X
C  E  I  Y  H  F  U  M  C  R  G  C  N  G  O  U  M  M  R  Z  Y  F
O  T  U  N  I  Z  M  V  U  O  J  N  E  E  Q  O  P  B  T  O  J  H
S  W  D  T  R  D  U  I  F  W  N  E  G  E  C  Z  M  C  B  M  U  H
M  E  P  J  Y  K  E  S  D  P  R  R  C  S  D  D  Z  C  E  G  K  Y
E  S  M  V  P  S  F  P  L  V  U  B  A  P  Z  F  O  I  Q  Y  B  A
T  B  C  Z  A  D  S  C  L  S  J  P  K  Y  I  R  B  T  A  B  C  O
I  O  P  O  A  H  B  M  C  A  S  S  U  E  G  H  O  Y  A  K  C  W
C  E  Z  F  P  P  A  I  D  L  C  M  R  M  I  A  A  H  T  L  O  Q
D  X  C  A  V  E  T  H  A  A  M  E  K  T  Z  E  R  Y  M  N  N  Z
E  A  B  W  I  S  O  C  A  M  P  J  B  Q  U  A  D  Q  N  L  T  W
R  G  J  N  A  C  I  F  G  P  S  B  O  O  K  F  C  D  W  M  R  P
M  C  I  L  P  D  U  V  P  B  U  D  F  B  N  P  E  Y  Q  G  O  B
A  B  P  R  E  T  N  T  S  R  Z  Z  O  N  S  E  R  Q  V  J  L  Y
T  F  N  M  Y  I  N  N  J  O  A  B  W  D  J  V  T  E  W  F  G  J
O  Q  P  A  M  O  I  X  I  O  G  C  V  O  C  R  I  H  Q  V  R  I
L  E  X  E  X  I  H  C  S  K  I  S  T  M  W  Z  F  X  I  G  O  N
O  V  O  P  U  L  F  L  U  C  A  Q  Z  I  T  K  I  Y  I  T  U  Y
G  G  H  K  A  T  A  I  M  D  C  Q  K  K  C  R  E  M  Z  Q  P  L
Y  U  B  U  Z  A  D  Z  R  U  S  O  O  J  J  E  D  K  J  C  M  T
U  E  M  X  F  R  E  M  W  Q  E  T  U  N  E  V  F  C  Q  N  N  B
F  Q  N  E  I  O  D  N  F  L  G  H  M  F  T  P  Y  B  D  J  L  L
```

SCOPE OF PRACTICE

Answer the following questions.

1. What are some of the noninvasive procedures done in a medical spa?

    _____

2. What are two names for an esthetician that works in the medical field?

    _____

3. When working in the medical field, you should always check with your state legislature
    for _____

4. What are the educational requirements in your state?

    _____

5. What are the various types of doctors that an esthetician can work with?

    a. _____

    b. _____

    c. _____

    d. _____

    e. _____

6. What is the difference between a cosmetic surgeon and a reconstructive surgeon?

    _____

    _____

    _____

    _____

    _____

7. What kind of medical practices can a medical aesthetics spa be associated with?

    _____

8. What are two types of nurses? _____

    _____

THE SCIENTIFIC METHOD

Answer the following questions.

1. All medical protocols are based on the _____ *a philosophy of reasoning that
    is based on first generating and then testing a* _____

2. Name the five steps of the scientific method.

a. _____

b. _____

c. _____

d. _____

e. _____

3. Explain what the term "control group" means.

_____

4. What is a placebo?

_____

_____

5. What is anecdotal evidence?

_____

_____

6. What does the acronym SOAP stand for? _____

7. How do you refer to the patrons of a medical spa? _____

25 MEDICAL TERMINOLOGY

Date: _____

Rating: _____

Text Pages: 672–687

HOW MEDICAL TERMINOLOGY WORKS

1. By knowing the meaning of a Greek or Latin _____, you can understand the meaning of an entire word. The use of _____ and _____ gives further clarity.

2. What does the suffix *-ology* mean? _____

3. What does the suffix *-graphy* mean? _____

4. To find the suffix of a word, isolate the different parts of the word. Look for the *o* or another

   _____.

WORD ANALYSIS

Write the root part of the word next to the word itself.

opthalmoscope   _____

polyneuropathy   _____

pathology   _____

intravenous   _____

leukocyte   _____

amniocentesis   _____

PLURALS

List the 10 common exceptions to basic plural rules.

1. _____

   _____

2. _____

   _____

3. _____

   _____

   _____

4. _____

   _____

5. _____

6. _____

7. _____

   _____

8. _____

9. _____

10. _____

ROOT WORDS

Write the meaning next to each root word.

1. acanth _____

2. anth _____

3. angi _____

4. bronchi _____

5. cele _____

6. blephar _____

7. ech _____

8. hydr _____

9. kine _____

10. lip _____

11. melan _____

12. derm _____

13. desm _____

14. cry; crym _____

15. aut _____

16. hem; hemat _____

17. micr _____

18. my; myo; myos _____

19. myel _____

20. nos _____

21. ox; oxy _____

22. path _____

23. phag _____

24. phleb _____

25. morph _____

26. phy _____

27. phot _____

28. phlact _____

29. phyll _____

30. pto _____

31. rhin; rhine _____

32. tachy _____

33. thorac _____

34. xer _____

35. alb _____

36. aur _____

37. capill _____

38. cervic _____

39. cut _____

40. flagell _____

41. fung _____

42. lamell _____

43. medi _____

44. nev _____

45. nutri _____

46. orb _____

47. pron _____

48. prur _____

49. rupt _____

50. strat _____

51. tact _____

52. termin _____

53. ven _____

54. vesic _____

55. vit _____

PREFIXES

Write the meaning next to each prefix.

1. a-; an- _____

2. ana- _____

3. anti- _____

4. cata- _____

5. dys- _____

6. endo- _____

7. epi- _____

8. hyper- _____

9. hypo- _____

10. meta- _____

11. para- _____

12. pro- _____

13. sym- _____

14. ante- _____

15. circum- _____

16. com-; con-; co- _____

17. contra- _____

18. intra- _____

19. infra- _____

20. juxta- _____

21. post- _____

22. pro- _____

23. sub- _____

24. trans- _____

25. ultra- _____

SUFFIXES

Write the meaning next to each suffix.

1. -iac _____

2. -ia

3. -is _____

4. -ism _____

5. -logy _____

6. -gen _____

7. -y _____

8. -plasty _____

9. -itis _____

10. -icle _____

11. -al _____

12. -ate _____

13. -ectomy _____

14. -emia _____

15. -iasis _____

16. -in; -ine _____

17. -ize _____

18. -phobia _____

19. -plasty _____

20. -stomy _____

21. -therapy _____

22. -tomy _____

23. -ency _____

24. -itious _____

PRONUNCIATION

How are the following letter combinations pronounced?

1. ph _____

2. ps _____

3. ch _____

4. mn _____

5. pt _____

6. pn _____

7. dys _____

8. gn _____

9. x _____

26 MEDICAL INTERVENTION

Date: _____

Rating: _____

Text Pages: 688–708

MEDICAL INTERVENTION AND THE ESTHETICIAN'S ROLE
_____

Answer the following questions.

1. Give one example of non-surgical aesthetics. _____

2. What are the two sides of medical esthetics? _____

3. With what does the esthetic side primarily deal? _____

4. About what type of medical procedures would an esthetician consult with a client?

    _____

5. What professionals can administer Botox or dermal fillers? _____

6. What information should an esthetician discuss in regard to dermal fillers?

    _____

    _____

7. With what should the esthetician be intimately familiar?

    _____

8. What is meant by the "durability" of products?

    _____

    _____

9. How do you choose the most durable product?

    _____

    _____

AN INTRODUCTION TO BOTOX
_____

Answer the following questions.

1. What are some of the complications with Botox? _____

    _____

2. In what areas would Botox be injected for wrinkles?

_____

_____

3. How long does Botox last? _____

4. What is eyelid ptosis?

_____

5. Up until recently, what conditions has Botox been able to treat?

_____

6. Botox is the product name for _____

7. List the indications for Botox:

a. _____

b. _____

c. _____

d. _____

e. _____

f. _____

g. _____

h. _____

i. _____

8. Use the words in the word bank to complete the following paragraph.

brow laxity   glabellar
droopiness   inexperienced
forehead   ptosis

"Forehead lines are the horizontal lines that are created when the brow is lifted. Treating the _____ can be one of the more challenging indications because the depth of the lines may be an indication of potential _____. Compete relaxation can be responsible for brow _____, especially in the hands of the _____ injector. When evaluating the brow for treatments, look for several key indicators: brow heaviness or _____, lid heaviness, _____ involvement, and depth of lines."

9. Where are the "crow's feet" located? _____

10. Where are the "marionette lines" located?

_____

11. What is another name for vertical lip lines? _____

12. What are the more serious yet uncommon adverse reactions associated with the use of Botox in the treatment of cervical dystonia and blepharoplasm?

a. _____

b. _____

c. _____

d. _____

AN INTRODUCTION TO DERMAL FILLERS

Answer the following questions.

1. What are the positive qualities to a perfect injectable material?

a. _____

b. _____

2. What are the possible drawbacks of an injectable filler?

a. _____

b. _____

c. _____

d. _____

e. _____

3. When it comes to injectable fillers, what is important to the client?

a. _____

b. _____

c. _____

d. _____

e. _____

f. _____

g. _____

4. What different natural products are dermal fillers made of?

a. _____

b. _____

c. _____

d. _____

e. _____

5. When was bovine collagen approved? _____

6. Where is bovine collagen derived from? _____

7. What are the drawbacks to Bovine Collagen?

a. _____

b. _____

8. Where is autologous collagen derived from? _____

9. What was the main problem with autologous collagen? _____

10. Fill in the missing words within this paragraph using the word bank below.

extracellular	perfect
hyaluronic acid	polysaccharide
hypoallergenic	structure-stabilizing
natural volume	

"While there are other injectables available (many of which we will discuss) _____ seems to hold the best hope for a _____ dermal filler. Meeting many of the criteria noted by professionals such as durability, and as a _____ found in human tissue it is _____ Hyaluronic acid exists in the _____ space and functions as a space-filling, _____ and cell-protective molecule. In other words hyaluronic acid is in part, responsible for the _____ found in youthful skin. It would seem to be a perfect solution for dermal filling."

11. Label the photographs as to what the indication is and what treatment would be the best.

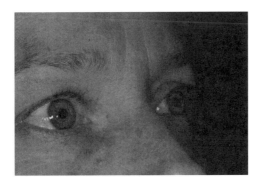

_____

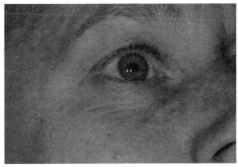

_____

_____

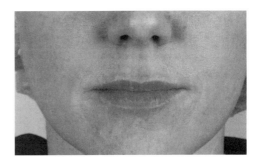

_____

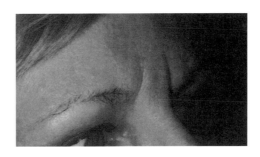

_____

_____

12. What are the brand names for bovine collagen? _____

13. What are the brand names for autologous collagen? _____

14. What is the trade name for the human collagen? _____

15. Fill in the blanks.

    a. Hyaluronic acid is a naturally occurring _____ (sugar).

    b. Fifty percent of the hyaluronic acid is housed in the _____.

    c. Hyaluronic acid's chemical makeup enables it to hold up to _____ in weight in water.

    d. The FDA-approved fillers with hyaluronic acid are _____.

    e. The non-FDA-approved fillers with hyaluronic acid are _____.

16. Fill in the missing information in this chart.

Name of Product	FDA Approval	Manufacturer
Hylaform	Yes	Inamed
Hylaform Plus		
Captique	Yes	
Restylane		Q-Med
Restylane Fine Line		
Perlane	No	
Juvederm	No	LEA Derm
Macrolane		
Dermalive		
DermaDeep		Dermatech
Matridur	No	Medical Aesthetic Supplies
Matridex		Medical Aesthetic Supplies
Achal		
Hylan Rofilan Gel	No	
Viscontour	No	Aventis Dermatology

17. Where is the hyaluronic acid that is in Hylaform Gel derived form?

_____

18. When was Restylane FDA approved? _____

19. What is the hyaluronic acid in Restylane cross-linked with? _____

20. What does NASHA stand for? _____

21. What treatments is Restylane popular for?

_____

_____

22. What is a common mistake when using dermal fillers in the lips? _____

INTRODUCTION TO SCLEROTHERAPY

Answer the following questions.

1. Use the words in the word bank to complete the paragraph below.

red, blue, or purple veins   valves
spider veins   varicose veins

"Dilated blood vessels, also known as _____, are a problem for many people.
They appear as _____ through the skin's surface, most often on the
lower extremities. As we age, these can also be found on the hands. These are a result of
the failure of _____ within the veins. Most often varicose veins—and especially
_____—are relatively harmless, even if they are unsightly."

2. Explain the three generalities of varicose veins.

a. Gender: _____

_____

_____

b. Geography: _____

_____

_____

c. Age: _____

_____

_____

3. How can the esthetician be helpful during sclerotherapy? _____

_____

4. What conditions would disqualify someone from having a sclerotherapy treatment?

a. _____

b. _____

c. _____

d. _____

e. _____

f. _____

g. _____

5. Explain the client preparation for sclerotherapy.

    _____

INTRODUCTION TO MEDICAL PEELS

Answer the following questions.

1. Explain what a chemical peel does. _____

    _____

2. What are the four levels of peeling?

    a. _____

    b. _____

    c. _____

    d. _____

3. What will chemical peeling help with? _____

4. List different types of peeling agents.

    a. _____

    b. _____

    c. _____

    d. _____

    e. _____

5. Glycolic comes from what plant? _____

6. In what strengths is glycolic available? _____

7. What does a Jessner's peel have in it? _____

    _____

8. What type of peel is a Jessner's peel? _____

9. From what does salicylic acid derive? _____

10. In what strengths is a salicylic acid peel available? _____

11. If someone has a salicylate toxicity, what would the symptoms be? _____
_____ .

12. In what strengths is a TCA peel available? _____

13. What is the most commonly recognized TCA peel? _____

14. How far deep into the skin does a TCA peel penetrate? _____
_____

OTHER SOLUTIONS

1. Fill in the missing information in the chart.

Treatment	These Treatments:	These Treatments Do Not:
Trichloracetic Acid Peels	Flatten scarring Reduce rhytides _____ Improve hyperpigmentation	_____ _____ _____ _____
Jessner's Solution and Glycolic Acid Peels	Reduce rhytides _____ _____	Reduce pore size _____ Remove telangiectases Remove deep scarring

2. What are the contraindications for chemical peeling?

_____

27 PLASTIC SURGERY PROCEDURES

Date: _____

Rating: _____

Text Pages: 709–731

FACE-LIFT (RHYTIDECTOMY) _____

Answer the following questions.

1. What is a rhytidectomy? _____

2. With what procedures is the rhytidectomy usually partnered? _____
   _____

3. Along with the rhytidectomy, what skin resurfacing procedures can be used to fine-tune
   the facial skin? _____

4. What will a rhytidectomy treat? _____
   _____
   _____

5. How many types of face-lift techniques are there? _____
   _____

6. Why do people that smoke need to quit smoking 1 to 2 weeks before the surgery?
   _____
   _____

7. Explain the thread lift. _____
   _____
   _____
   _____
   _____

8. What does the thread lift treat? _____
   _____

9. How long does this procedure take? _____

FOREHEAD-LIFT (BROW-LIFT)

Answer the following questions.

1. What does a forehead-lift treat? _____

2. What other surgeries might be performed at the same time to complement the forehead-lift? _____

3. What are the two main surgical techniques for the forehead-lift? _____

4. How is the first technique performed? _____

5. How is the second technique performed? _____

6. Where is the incision in the classic forehead-lift? _____

EYE LIFT (BLEPHAROPLASTY)

Answer the following questions.

1. What is a blepharoplasty? _____

2. How many were performed in 2003? _____

3. What would a blepharoplasty treat? _____

4. What symptoms are not treated by a blepharoplasty? _____

5. What information is obtained prior to a blepharoplasty? _____

6. Which medical conditions would make the surgery risky? _____

7. Describe the incision process in the case of altering the upper eyelids. _____

8. Describe the incision process in the case of altering the lower eyelids. _____

_____

_____

9. What is a transconjunctival blepharoplasty? _____

_____

10. What is photophobia and when might it occur? _____

_____

NOSE JOB (RHINOPLASTY)

Answer the following questions.

1. What is a rhinoplasty? _____

2. Give an example of reconstructive rhinoplasty. _____

_____

3. What can contribute to nasal airway obstruction? _____

_____

4. Give an example of cosmetic rhinoplasty. _____

_____

5. What other surgeries can be performed with rhinoplasty? _____

6. Describe a rhinoplasty procedure. _____

_____

_____

_____

7. What can influence the outcome of the surgery? _____

_____

_____

_____

8. What are the two types of rhinoplasty? _____

FACIAL IMPLANTS

Answer the following questions.

1. What are a few examples of facial implants?

_____

2. What procedures can a facial implant be partnered with?

_____

3. Describe a facial implant procedure.

_____

_____

_____

_____

_____

_____

BREAST IMPLANTS (AUGMENTATION MAMMAPLASTY)

Answer the following questions.

1. What is the technical name for breast implants?

_____

2. Why do women get breast implants?

_____

_____

3. Describe a breast implant surgery.

_____

_____

_____

4. Why would a woman need to postpone breast implant surgery?

_____

5. What happens before the procedure?

_____

_____

_____

_____

6. What type of breast cancer screening might happen prior to a procedure?

_____

BREAST-LIFT (MASTOPEXY)

Answer the following questions.

1. Who is a good candidate for a breast-lift?

_____

_____

_____

2. A breast-lift involves what types of incisions?

_____

3. What are the pre-procedure considerations of this surgery?

_____

_____

BREAST REDUCTION (REDUCTION MAMMAPLASTY)

Answer the following questions.

1. Who are good candidates for breast reduction?

_____

_____

2. What medical symptoms might a woman have from having pendulous breasts?

a. _____

b. _____

c. _____

d. _____

e. _____

f. _____

g. _____

h. _____

i. _____

j. _____

3. How is the surgery different than mastopexy?

_____

_____

4. What type of pre-procedure considerations should there be?

_____

_____

_____

BREAST RECONSTRUCTION

Answer the following questions.

1. Who is a good candidate for breast reconstruction?

    _____

2. Why should clients who smoke quit prior to the procedure?

    _____

3. Where is an implant inserted?

    _____

4. How does a surgeon perform a skin expansion plus breast implant procedure?

    _____

    _____

    _____

5. Describe a distant or flap reconstruction.

    _____

    _____

    _____

    _____

6. Describe a musculocutaneous flap.

    _____

    _____

    _____

    _____

    _____

7. Describe the free flap.

    _____

    _____

    _____

    _____

    _____

8. Explain postoperative activity after a breast implant procedure.

    _____

    _____

    _____

    _____

    _____

9. What risks are involved in breast reconstruction?

_____

TUMMY TUCK (ABDOMINOPLASTY)

Answer the following questions.

1. What is the technical name for tummy tuck? _____

2. What benefits does a tummy tuck offer?

_____

3. What is another surgery that would compliment a tummy tuck? _____

4. What are the pre-procedure considerations?

_____

_____

_____

_____

5. Describe a miniabdominoplasty.

_____

_____

_____

_____

_____

_____

6. Describe a full abdominoplasty.

_____

_____

_____

_____

_____

_____

_____

_____

LIPOSUCTION (SUCTION-ASSISTED LIPOPLASTY)

Answer the following questions.

1. What are the other names for liposuction?

_____

2.   In what areas would a patient receive liposuction?

_____

_____

3.   What is cellulite?

_____

_____

_____

4.   What is the name of the tool used to perform liposuction? _____

5.   What are the pre-procedure considerations?

_____

PUTTING IT ALL TOGETHER

Draw a line from the term to its definition.

rhinoplasty	alters the shape of the breast
circumareolar	the top profile of the nose
bariatric surgery	stretch marks
liposuction	refers to a nose job
mammaplasty	refers to a tummy tuck
rhytidectomy	refers to eyelid surgery
blepharoplasty	refers to a face-lift
dorsum	refers to a breast-lift
abdominoplasty	refers to the circumference of the areola
striae distensae	removing stubborn areas of fat
mastopexy	gastric bypass surgery

28 THE ESTHETICIAN'S ROLE IN PRE- AND POST-MEDICAL TREATMENTS

Date: _____

Rating: _____

Text Pages: 732–745

PRE-MEDICAL OR LASER INTERVENTION PROCEDURES

Find the following terms in the word search puzzle below.

ablative	Famir
Aquaphor	liposuction
Cipro	lymphatic
facial	rosacea

```
A  C  B  I  N  D  J  P  T  J  X  Y  Q  O  N  L  D  P  B  A
B  B  P  R  D  D  S  O  A  L  H  Z  W  D  X  I  K  I  S  J
L  Z  S  P  Q  P  Y  X  J  Q  Q  R  Q  I  W  X  E  K  Q  M
A  D  F  V  H  P  M  C  L  Y  M  P  H  A  T  I  C  J  M  P
T  P  L  V  A  D  C  I  R  Q  J  S  C  V  O  X  H  E  Q  L
I  G  G  K  H  H  G  E  I  Q  B  P  Y  R  T  G  J  N  L  L
V  C  L  F  L  E  S  E  T  P  M  P  Y  Q  V  T  H  T  T  O
E  V  V  I  I  E  S  E  B  B  N  A  F  Z  A  Z  Q  F  P  N
R  W  W  Q  P  J  M  H  G  H  H  Y  F  L  K  Q  R  M  G  C
Q  P  K  X  X  O  N  K  P  X  P  W  H  H  I  E  Z  H  J  A
W  G  N  Z  H  O  S  I  I  P  Z  O  A  R  U  E  I  W  M  E
C  U  K  R  G  F  O  U  H  K  N  U  O  P  F  N  U  U  T  C
Z  J  A  V  I  A  T  W  C  R  T  H  W  X  V  F  F  C  Z  A
B  R  U  V  O  C  J  W  U  T  P  X  W  T  X  F  H  D  K  S
J  Q  L  R  W  I  Y  Y  O  A  I  S  L  K  B  K  Q  O  P  O
I  F  P  V  N  A  Z  O  U  W  G  O  V  A  C  K  Y  T  C  R
B  I  T  Q  Z  L  E  Q  N  Q  M  K  N  Z  C  V  J  N  H  C
C  L  T  Z  P  C  A  S  H  Z  W  H  B  I  K  K  S  L  R  T
```

1.   How will the skin react to the procedure if the skin is in good condition prior to the procedure?

_____

2.   Name the various facial plastic surgeries.

_____

3.   What are various types of ablative laser procedures?

_____

4.   How does the skin react to laser procedures?

_____

5.   What should be happening 8 weeks prior to a laser treatment?

_____

6.   What determines the treatment plan?

_____

_____

7.   List clinic treatments that an esthetician can perform.

a.   _____

b.   _____

c.   _____

d.   _____

e.   _____

f.   _____

g.   _____

8.   Use the words in the word bank to complete the paragraph below.

AHA   progressively
BHA   retinoic acid
exfoliating   salicylic acid
Jessner's   skin lightening
traumatizing

"These peels include _____ , _____ , retinoic acid, _____ , or
_____ ; select a peel starting with the lowest concentration and gradually increase in
strength as the client tolerates. These treatments help to stimulate the home-care program by
_____ the upper layers of the epidermis and serve as an additional _____
measure. It is important to make sure the client stops using home-care AHAs, _____ ,
or scrubs 2 to 3 days before and 3 to 5 days after a peel, depending on its strength. Follow

manufacturer's guidelines and avoid being too aggressive, which may result in _____ the skin. This is your time to use your experience, education and critical thinking skills to improve the client's skin; with your help, his or her skin can become _____ better in tone and texture and the client will not have to deal with possible side effects or complications."

9. Describe microdermabrasion.

_____

_____

_____

10. What should a client stop using prior to a microdermabrasion treatment?

_____

_____

11. Who should not receive a microdermabrasion treatment?

_____

_____

ENZYMES

Answer the following questions.

1. What type of enzymes are there?

    a. _____

    b. _____

    c. _____

    d. _____

2. Where does the enzyme papain come from? _____

3. What benefits do enzymes offer?

    _____

4. Describe ultrasonic technology.

    _____

    _____

5. How does the ultrasonic treatment differ from microdermabrasion?

    _____

6. What is the exfoliation stage called? _____

7. What is the hydrating stage called? _____

8. During which stage would beneficial serums penetrate? _____

9. Describe microcurrent facial toning:

_____

_____

10. How often would a client need to receive microcurrent facial toning treatments?

_____

11. Describe lymph drainage.

_____

_____

12. What are the benefits of lymph drainage?

_____

13. When is lymph drainage commonly performed?

_____

PRE-SURGICAL HOME CARE

Answer the following questions.

1. Prior to a procedure, what should the client be doing at home?

_____

2. What would a pre-laser home-care kit focus on? _____

3. List the items in a pre-laser home care kit.

a. _____

b. _____

c. _____

d. _____

e. _____

4. What are the home-care directions for the morning?

a. _____

b. _____

c. _____

d. _____

5. What are the home-care directions for the evening?

a. _____

b. _____

c. _____

d. _____

6. Use the words in the word bank to complete the paragraph below.

classification   optimum
exfoliate   protect
face-lift   treatment plans
laser resurfacing

"As with _____ or other cosmetic procedure, the client will tolerate the post-surgical phase much better if his or her skin is in _____ condition. If the client is having a combination of procedures—such as a _____ and laser resurfacing—you need to combine both _____ . Depending on skin type and _____ , clients need to use, at a minimum, products designed to _____ , hydrate, condition, and _____ ."

7. Name the key ingredients in the following products.

a. Cleansers: _____

b. Exfoliators: _____

c. Hydrators/moisturizers: _____

_____

d. Eye creams: _____

e. Sunscreen: _____

AFTER CO_2/ERBIUM ND:YAG LASER RESURFACING

Explain what happens during the first 5 days after the procedure: _____

_____

_____

_____

_____
_____
_____
_____
_____
_____

Explain what happens during days 5 to 10 after the procedure: _____

_____
_____
_____
_____
_____
_____
_____
_____

Days 10 to 30 after the procedure: _____

_____
_____
_____

One month post-laser: _____

_____
_____
_____

AFTER A RHYTIDECTOMY OR FACE-LIFT

Explain what happens during the first week after surgery: _____

_____
_____
_____
_____
_____
_____
_____
_____
_____

Days 8 to 15 after surgery: _____

_____
_____
_____

_____

2 weeks after surgery: _____

_____

_____

_____

_____

_____

_____

3 weeks or more after surgery: _____

_____

_____

_____

_____

BLEPHAROPLASTY

Explain what happens during days 1 to 7 after surgery: _____

_____

_____

_____

_____

_____

_____

_____

_____

Days 7 to 12 after surgery: _____

_____

_____

2 to 3 weeks after surgery: _____

_____

_____

2 to 6 months after surgery: _____

_____

_____

JOWL/NECK/CHIN LIPOSUCTION

Explain what happens 1 to 3 days after surgery: _____

_____

_____

_____

_____

_____

_____

Day 4 to 4 weeks after surgery: _____

_____

_____

_____

_____

_____

_____

_____

_____

4 weeks or more after surgery: _____

_____

_____

_____

_____

WHEN TO REFER BACK TO A PHYSICIAN

Answer the following questions.

1. When would a consultation with a physician be needed? _____

    _____

    _____ you should immediately refer that client to his or her
    physician for evaluation. Also, patients can have **contact dermatitis** or an **allergic reaction**
    to topical skin preparations or ointments. If any of these indicators are present, do not
    perform any procedures without a physician's approval.

2.   Draw a line matching the following terms to their definitions.

allergic reaction   Skin lightener

blepharoplasty   Eyelid surgery

collagen shrinkage   Removal of fatty deposits

contact dermatitis   Antiviral medication

Famvir   Formation of new epidermis

hydroquinone   Using a CO_2 or Erbium laser

laser resurfacing   A localized skin reaction caused from contact with a substance

liposuction   An abnormal reaction and hypersensitivity

reepithelization   Thermal heating can break down the collagen

29 FINANCIAL BUSINESS SKILLS

Date: _____

Rating: _____

Text Pages: 747–763

CALCULATING BUSINESS RISK

Answer the following questions.

1. What does *risk* refer to? _____

   _____

2. What is a business plan? _____

   _____

   _____

THE BUSINESS PLAN

1. Fill in the missing steps in this business plan.

I. Executive Summary

    a. _____

    b. _____

       _____

    c. _____

II. Marketing Strategy

    a. _____

    b. _____

    c. _____

    d. _____

    e. _____

       _____

III. Strategic Design and Development

    a. _____

    b. _____

    c. _____

    d. _____

    e. _____

    f. _____

IV. Operations

    a. _____
      _____

    b. _____

    c. _____

    d. _____

    e. _____

    f. _____

    g. _____

    h. _____
      _____
      _____

V. Financial Information

    a. _____

    b. _____

    c. _____

    d. _____

    e. _____
      _____

    f. _____
      _____

g. _____

h. _____

2. What should an executive summary state? _____

_____

3. What should the marketing plan section state? _____

_____

_____

4. What should the strategic design and development plan state? _____

_____

_____

_____

_____

5. What should the operations plan state? _____

_____

_____

_____

_____

_____

6. What should the financial plan state? _____

_____

_____

7. What should the conclusion section state? _____

_____

_____

_____

FINANCIAL PLANNING

Answer the following questions.

1. What does *capital* mean? _____

_____

2. What is a venture capitalist? _____

_____

3. What is a promissory note? _____

_____

4. What is the SBA and what does it do? _____

    _____

5. What resources does the SBA offer? _____

    _____

FINANCIAL TOOLS

Answer the following questions.

1. What are the financial tools designed to help you manage finances with your
    accountant? _____

2. What is a balance sheet? _____

    _____

3. What are assets? _____

4. What are liabilities? _____

    _____

5. What is owner's equity? _____

    _____

    _____

6. What is an income statement? _____

    _____

    _____

    _____

7. How do you total up the net profit? _____

    _____

8. What is the cash flow statement? _____

    _____

9. What is a break-even analysis? _____

    _____

PROTECTING BUSINESS ASSETS

Answer the following questions.

1. What is risk management? _____

2. What type of insurance should you have?

    a. _____

    b. _____

    c. _____

    d. _____

    e. _____

    f. _____

    g. _____

EMPLOYEE COMPENSATION

Answer the following questions.

1. What are the different ways to compensate employees?

    a. _____

    b. _____

    c. _____

2. How should you report tips to the IRS? _____

3. What is an independent contractor? _____

    _____

4. What are the three general categories that determine Independent Contractor status?

    a. _____

    b. _____

    c. _____

5. Where can you find more information on these three categories? _____

    _____

    _____

6. If you are an independent contractor, who pays your taxes? _____

UNDERSTANDING THE IRS

Answer the following questions.

1. What is a Social Security Number? _____

2. What is an Employer Identification Number? _____
   _____

3. What is an Individual Tax Identification Number? _____
   _____
   _____

4. What is the W-4 form for? _____
   _____

5. What is the W-2 form for? _____
   _____
   _____

6. What is the I-9 form for? _____
   _____

7. What tax form does an independent contractor receive? _____

8. By what date do taxes need to be paid? _____

9. What are the names of the payroll tax deductions? _____
   _____

10. What other very important tax are employers responsible for paying? _____
    _____

11. What is a self-employment tax? _____
    _____
    _____

12. If you make estimated payments four times a year, what form should you use?
    _____

13. Define resale tax. _____

14. What is the deferred income tax? _____
    _____
    _____

15. Explain tax penalties. _____

_____

_____

PUTTING IT ALL TOGETHER

Answer the following questions. Then look for the answers in the word search on the following page.

It is a type of note that defines the terms of a loan. _____

It is the chance of incurring some type of harm. _____

It is a statement that indicates how much money is flowing in and out of a business on a regular basis. _____

It provides protection against business casualties. _____

It is the type of profit that is the total amount of money a business takes in from the sale of products and services. _____

If you have your own business, you are an _____ contractor.

It is the amount of money invested in a business. _____

It is due by April 15th. _____

It is a type of analysis that states the point at which all costs are covered and your business begins to earn a profit. _____

It is what provides a financial overview of a business at a given point in time in terms of its assets and liabilities. _____

```
A D M B T N W R H W H A Z O C J N I H R
X X X W W H Z C E S Z U X D X T N M D S
W W V E K I A W S V P C R D U D Q P P X
G R O S S P K D D P X H K I E I E X H S
X P X H I T V C E D S G M P Q N A C K W
B V A T T Q Y M I E L R E S H S O A B S
K A A Y I X Y N L T H N L W G U K S X T
L L L L W X C R L H D T T L T R M H L G
O O N A V W A B O E S L D I B A S F T R
X K J E N C B D N S Y D U U P N V L L E
G O L K F C Q T E L S A L W H C Y O D H
U H I Z B M E X V P O I J U Z E L W O E
C K G V H L A S R Z I U M O Q V A K S H
M B W D I T X W H Z R G E O P O S J E V
T I U N E V E K A E R B E T R I G F X C
K P C G J Z J A N R E O J D R P Z R X H
F C V A W V S Y S A O T C K F H K V C V
H E M X J R U Q N R Y R R E G C S D E E
M K A W Q Z F L Y M X Y L E R J X K Y E
Y U S I S Z G J D D P R L T Y T P C P U
```

30 MARKETING

Date: _____

Rating: _____

Text Pages: 764–779

THE DEFINITION OF MARKETING

Answer the following questions.

1. Explain the basic principles of marketing. _____
    _____

2. What happens during the process of marketing? _____
    _____

3. What are the Four Ps in Marketing? _____

4. What does *Product* mean? _____
    _____
    _____
    _____

5. What does the business of skin care sell? _____
    _____

6. Use the following words to complete the paragraph below.

    brand recognition   medical aesthetic facilities
    good public relations   positive
    image   "product"

    "Image is another significant factor that helps business owners to establish what is referred to as _____. Today's skin care businesses may be housed in any number of facilities, including beauty salons, separate skin care salons, spa-and-salon combinations, or _____ . Before you can develop a solid marketing plan, you must decide on the main focus of your business and establish a brand name that embodies the _____ you wish to project. There are other aspects of branding that you should not overlook, such as a _____ program, which will help you to develop a _____ public image. This is all part of developing your _____"

7. What is one thing that you should consider when it comes to pricing? _____

_____

_____

8. What should your pricing strategy be based on? _____

_____

9. What is a promotion? _____

_____

10. What forms of communication are involved in promotion?

    a. _____

    b. _____

    c. _____

    d. _____

    e. _____

    f. _____

11. To what does *Place* refer? _____

_____

_____

_____

_____

_____

CUSTOMER VALUE

Answer the following questions.

1. What is a consumer? _____

2. What is a seller? _____

_____

3. What are demographics? _____

_____

_____

_____

4. Where is one place you can find demographic information? _____

5. Gathering demographic information is an important part of the marketing process. What are the demographics around your school or salon? _____

_____

Ages: _____

Sex: _____

Income: _____

Education level: _____

Spending habits: _____

6. Given the demographics in your area, what skin care products could you sell easily to every client? _____

CUSTOMER RELATIONSHIP MANAGEMENT

Answer the following questions.

1. In what do smart business owners invest a great deal of time? _____

_____

_____

2. Create a moisturizing product. It can contain various beneficial ingredients and can be priced at any range. Describe the product below. _____

_____

_____

What are its benefits? _____

What is the price? _____

Ask 10 people if they would buy this product and how much they would spend.

Record your results.

Person #1 _____

Person #2 _____

Person #3 _____

Person #4 _____

Person #5 _____

Person #6 _____

Person #7 _____

Person #8 _____

Person #9 _____

Person #10 _____

3. What would a total quality management program include? _____

    _____

    _____

    _____

4. Give an example of good customer service that you have had in the past.

    _____

5. What is one tool you can use to help you continually evaluate your skin care methods?

    _____

THE PROMOTION MIX

Answer the following questions.

1. What are different ways you can promote your business?

    a. _____

    b. _____

    c. _____

    d. _____

    e. _____

    f. _____

2. As you establish the best methods for promoting your business, it is often helpful to think in what terms? _____

ADVERTISING

Describe each of the following methods of advertising.

1. Classified Ads: _____
    _____
    _____
    _____
    _____

2. Newspaper ads: _____
    _____
    _____
    _____
    _____

3. Magazine ads: _____
    _____
    _____
    _____
    _____

4. Radio and television ads: _____
    _____
    _____
    _____
    _____

5. Direct mail ads: _____
    _____
    _____
    _____
    _____
    _____

6. Activity: Write out your ad for your salon.

PUBLIC RELATIONS

1. List some public relations pieces you can create for a business.

   a. _____

   b. _____

   c. _____

2. What is the benefit of gaining publicity? _____

   _____

3. What are some ways you can gain publicity?

   a. _____

   b. _____

   c. _____

   d. _____

   e. _____

   f. _____

4. What type of publicity events can you do for your salon or school in your area?

DIRECT MARKETING

Answer the following questions.

1. Explain direct marketing: _____

   _____

2. What are the two important factors in direct marketing? _____

3. Create your own direct mail advertising piece. _____

   _____

PERSONAL SELLING

Answer the following questions.

1. What is personal selling? _____
   _____

2. What does personal selling require? _____

SALES PROMOTIONS

Answer the following questions.

1. What are the common types of sales promotions? _____
   _____
   _____

2. What are some creative ways you can bring attention to various salon treatments and products? _____
   _____
   _____
   _____

3. Describe how you would structure a frequent customer/membership program.
   _____

THE MARKETING PLAN

Answer the following questions.

1. Your marketing plan should provide a detailed account of all of the marketing methods you will use to achieve your goals. List those marketing methods.

   a. _____

   b. _____

   c. _____

   d. _____

   e. _____

f. _____

g. _____

2. What are the five primary objectives to consider in marketing skin care?

a. _____

b. _____

c. _____

d. _____

e. _____

3. What should be an ongoing expense in your business? _____

THE BROCHURE, OR MENU OF SERVICES

Answer the following questions.

1. Describe a brochure. _____

    _____

    _____

    _____

    _____

2. The brochure should be well written, organized, and _____

3. The brochure should be divided into _____

4. Draw up a brochure of your own. List and describe at least five services you would perform.

THE INTERNET

Answer the following questions.

1. What is the Internet? _____

    _____

2. Besides having a Web site, what else can you use the Internet for? _____

    _____

_____

_____

3.   What is the primary goal of any Web site? _____

_____

THE USE OF TECHNOLOGY

Answer the following questions.

1.   What can a good salon software program offer? _____

_____

_____

2.   Why would you need to track an employee's sales? _____

3.   List automatic business builders.

a.   _____

b.   _____

c.   _____

d.   _____

e.   _____

f.   _____

MARKETING RESPONSIBLY

Which government agencies oversee marketing practices and what do they oversee?

a.   _____

b.   _____

_____

c.   _____

_____

PUTTING IT ALL TOGETHER

Find the chapter's key words below within the word search.

brochure
demographic
Internet
marketing
menu
place

price
product
promotion
publicity
services

```
Y  B  C  D  Z  E  L  O  O  G  L  S  P  J  V  O  N  O  K  L
J  E  Q  X  D  I  M  E  H  V  A  H  O  Z  L  C  C  C  Q  J
R  W  T  Y  R  I  G  T  T  D  G  U  G  A  R  I  Y  I  P  L
J  S  W  U  R  J  G  Y  C  Y  M  H  T  O  K  U  M  N  S  U
S  P  P  R  O  D  U  C  T  N  P  U  B  L  I  C  I  T  Y  P
T  O  R  O  R  I  L  M  E  N  U  O  X  E  Q  W  U  E  S  P
D  E  M  O  G  R  A  P  H  I  C  F  X  R  W  P  V  R  P  R
L  P  Z  Q  M  X  X  N  T  N  W  R  Y  V  M  L  W  N  V  S
E  R  G  E  Q  O  L  E  N  F  S  P  K  W  A  A  R  E  H  S
W  G  T  X  N  X  T  N  T  N  J  N  Z  E  R  C  Z  T  N  F
U  N  Z  Z  D  A  W  I  U  A  R  C  R  V  K  E  H  Q  T  M
F  S  Z  K  M  L  R  I  O  W  G  U  L  Z  E  B  R  N  K  X
L  A  M  P  B  L  A  A  U  N  H  L  S  Q  T  D  F  K  C  K
N  Q  M  R  H  I  C  L  B  C  R  N  L  S  I  L  O  O  X  Z
L  P  Y  Y  R  V  U  V  O  E  F  U  O  B  N  E  E  H  E  Z
S  Q  R  V  W  O  K  R  F  C  K  L  F  F  G  C  S  C  O  M
V  Z  C  J  D  U  B  N  W  D  R  O  R  M  L  O  I  N  Q  L
I  M  I  E  R  X  T  S  W  X  N  K  U  Z  K  R  K  H  O  H
Z  J  Z  F  W  J  B  R  D  A  P  Q  F  M  P  U  G  K  C  P
Z  Y  W  D  X  B  B  S  E  R  V  I  C  E  S  M  Z  M  L  I
```